D1467694

Here's the Deal

Here's the Deal

How the McCoys Built America's Most
Admired  Acquisition at a Time

John B. McCoy

with Jeff Sheban

Foreword by Jamie Dimon

ORANGE *frazer* PRESS
Wilmington, Ohio

Published for the author by:
Orange Frazer Press
P.O. Box 214
Wilmington, OH 45177
Telephone: 937.382.3196 for price
and shipping information.
Website: www.orangefrazer.com

Book and cover design: Alyson Rua and Orange Frazer Press

Library of Congress Control Number: 2017958437

First Printing

Acknowledgments

While the McCoy and Bank One stories were generations in the making, creating this book was a relative breeze—thanks to so many people who helped along the way.

Let me start with a huge round of applause for collaborator Jeff Sheban. He made the book what it is. Jeff took the time to understand the characters and events and to portray them accurately and with the right amount of flair. He truly helped me to tell the story of the McCoys and deserves the credit for making the book so readable.

Bill Boardman and Bob Walter were invaluable sources and helped improve the book's accuracy; former *Columbus Dispatch* Editor and Associate Publisher, Mike Curtin, provided insightful thoughts and directions; Kevin Mayhood did research on the McCoy family; Linda Deitch of *The Dispatch* retrieved many images for our consideration and J.P. Morgan Chase archivists, Nancy Palley and Jean Elliott, kindly granted access to their unique collection. Their boss, Jamie Dimon, was kind enough to reflect on my family in his foreword.

I am grateful for the dedicated staff at Orange Frazer Press, especially the dynamic mother-daughter team of Marcy and Sarah Hawley, who kept their cool and made a manuscript a book.

Where would I be without my long-time secretary Sandy Anderson, who keeps the trains running on time, and my wonderful sister Jinny McCoy, who keeps and remembers everything that I forget? Let me answer: I'd be lost. Finally, for their help and patience, thanks to my wife and children for always being there for me—even when I couldn't always be there for them. I owe you the world, especially my dear Jane. It never would have happened without you.

Contents

Foreword by Jamie Dimon

*A*s chairman, president, and chief executive officer of JPMorgan Chase, I've had the opportunity to know the McCoy family since shortly after my unceremonious defenestration at Citigroup, when then-Bank One CEO John B. McCoy called me out of the blue and said he wanted to meet me the next time he came to New York. We met at the Carlyle Hotel in late 1998 and had an engaging, interesting, fun meeting. While we did speak about Bank One a bit, I was not completely sure why he had arranged the meeting. Several months later, I was contacted by the search committee that was seeking a successor to John. Somehow, after a series of meetings and interviews, they made an unconventional bet on me and decided I was the man for the job.

My introduction to Bank One and the McCoys came from Harvard Business School case studies that focused on an innovative regional bank based in Columbus, Ohio. The material showcased Bank One's aggressive M&A and expansion, and its innovation around ATMs, credit and debit cards, and customer service. John G. McCoy and John B. McCoy had built a regional powerhouse from a bank of very little consequence. It was really quite extraordinary.

This book is a fascinating retelling of the McCoy and Bank One stories, which are very much one and the same. Starting with John H. McCoy, a Depression-era oilman turned banker who landed at City National Bank & Trust in Columbus, forerunner to Bank One, and literally outworked the more established competition; to his son John G. McCoy, an innovator who had the vision to see that consumer banking and customer service were the wave of the future; to John B. McCoy, a skillful tactician who orchestrated more than

100 bank acquisitions to create a regional banking powerhouse that remains a cornerstone of today's JPMorgan Chase. Bank One's roots account for roughly 40 percent of the current JPMorgan Chase, arguably one of the best banks in the world—spanning the globe and serving as a testament to the trials and tribulations of the McCoys and all of our other predecessors.

John G. McCoy, who took advantage of liberalizing state banking laws to expand throughout Ohio, was a banking legend and mentor to many, including me. We host periodic dinners to thank and recognize the former directors of our predecessor firms. At the one and only dinner John G. could attend (he was in a wheelchair at the time), we honored him by mounting his portrait in the board room of our New York headquarters, right next to the portrait of our founder, J.P. Morgan himself.

After succeeding John B. as CEO of Bank One, not once did I get anything but constructive ideas and unflinching support as I worked to restore Bank One to its former glory. And, over time, we were able to reinstitute their innovative ways and begin to grow the company again. It has been my pleasure to get to know the whole McCoy family, including John B. McCoy's wonderful wife Jane and their children. I remain in touch with John B. to this day.

Certain things never go out of style in business—hard work, good ideas and great execution among the most important. It's a simple formula when you read it in a book or in a case study. Putting it into practice is quite another thing. For three generations, the McCoys exhibited the passion, determination and willingness to be bold and to be different. That's what set them apart and that is how they changed the face of banking in this country. I am honored to follow in that tradition.

Preface

*J*ohn McCoy is an exceedingly ordinary name. There are thousands of John McCoys going about their business all over the world. But in banking circles, John McCoy is an extraordinary name, a mark of excellence in its association with Bank One (now part of JPMorgan Chase) and its predecessor institution, City National Bank & Trust of Columbus, Ohio. To thank for that, I have my grandfather, John H. McCoy, who salvaged a weak number three bank in Columbus and made it a scrappy competitor, and father, John G. McCoy, who pioneered industry firsts including credit cards and drive-up windows and laid the groundwork for what would become a truly national bank.

(*A quick note about our family naming convention.* To preserve our genealogy, the first-born male in each family is John, followed by his mother's maiden name. I'm John Bonnet McCoy, in honor of my mother, Jeanne Bonnet McCoy. My eldest son is John Taylor McCoy, after my wife Jane Taylor McCoy. His son is John Harrill, after his mother Anna Harrill McCoy. I love the tradition and have always thought it superior to being John the 5th or Henry the 8th, as the case may be. Hopefully, no one marries a Hatfield!)

As the third John McCoy to run Bank One or City National, I was always keenly aware of the need to live up to the expectations of such a great family name and legacy. It was an awesome responsibility that was both an advantage and a weight that followed me throughout a thirty-year banking career.

While all the Columbus McCoys had banking in common, each was his own man and a product of his times. My grandfather navigated the Great

Depression as both a bank regulator and president; my father helped change the face of banking in Ohio. Just as they were the right bankers for their eras, I set out to be the best banker for my generation and enjoyed some measure of success in creating the nation's fifth-largest financial institution through organic growth and more than 100 acquisitions. While extremely proud of my father and grandfather, and grateful for the strong foundation they laid, I set out to plot my own course as a son, husband, father and ultimately, bank president and CEO.

This is a book about that journey—equal parts family history, corporate history and personal story. But most of all, it's intended to be a tribute to all those who had a hand in creating what *The New York Times* once called "The best little bank in America," and now such an important part of JP Morgan Chase. These are their stories, as much as my own.

Introduction

People often ask me if I was destined to be a banker, or whether the career was forced upon me, considering that my father and grandfather both had run the same bank. The short answer to both is no. But I learned early on that I was well-suited for business and for building things.

My first real exposure to business came at a somewhat unlikely time and place—my sophomore year of college. I attended Williams College in Williamstown, Massachusetts, a wonderful liberal arts college where I majored in history. The story begins in the summer after my freshman year, when I traveled by passenger ship to Europe with a college friend. Our goal was to "see Europe on $5 a day," a popular (if fanciful) notion at the time. Neither one of us had very much money to spend, so we were thrilled to discover as we steamed out of New York harbor that Heineken beers were 10 cents a bottle—every college student's dream. Let's just say that we got our money's worth on that seven-day journey.

We joined up with two other classmates in Amsterdam, rented a VW van and began our adventure. While I had pre-purchased a return flight for $280, the liner had been so much fun that I was thinking about cashing in my plane ticket so I could purchase a return trip by boat. That was the plan, anyhow.

By the time we reached Pisa, Italy, money was running low. We also discovered that the tourist-class liner tickets we wanted were sold out, and that the remaining first-class tickets were more than we could afford. So we did what any college students would do—we went to a bar to formulate a strategy.

It was there we bumped into Jeffrey Feinstein, an American travel agent with Garber Travel, who needed help the next day getting a tour group from the airport to its hotel. He was in a bind and we needed some money, so we had a deal.

The group turned out to be 200 American dental hygienists, which only added to the fun. Feinstein asked me if I'd like to help with other groups, offering to pay my expenses and buy me a first-class boat ticket when it was time to go home. I agreed, split up with my friends and headed to Rome and then Paris for my new job as a European tour guide and logistics expert.

Feinstein and I became friends. One day I told him it was a shame more students couldn't afford to visit Europe because of the cost of transportation. That got him thinking, and he came up with the idea to charter planes for student travel. It would be my job to fill them up. In those days only non-profit groups could charter a plane, so when I returned to the U.S., we formed the non-profit National Collegiate Club with this noble mission statement: "For the betterment of student understanding around the world." Father arranged for a Columbus law firm to help draw up legal documents.

Back at Williamstown for my sophomore year, I went to a bank as advised by the lawyers to open a "client trust fund" account for the National

◄ *Previous page:* My grandfather and U.S. Navy officer John G. McCoy cradles me before shipping out in 1943. This photo was likely taken in my grandfather's *(left)* back yard.

Here's the Deal

Collegiate Club. This was a very specialized account—one intended to serve as a custodial account for other people's money—and you could tell the bank clerk was surprised to be doing this on behalf of a college kid in blue jeans.

Then he asked what amount I'd like to open the account with. I reached into my pocket and pulled out all I had—a $5 bill—and handed it over. Now he was *really* confused!

With the plans drawn up and the account opened, we got to work. Mainly by word of mouth we started to enlist helpers in several New England and Virginia colleges to distribute newsletters and sign up students for trips to Europe and the Caribbean. The cost to join the club was $10, and my campus representatives could earn a free trip after selling ten packages.

The venture was successful beyond our wildest dreams. Within six months there was more than $500,000 in the account. Garber Travel made the lion's share of profits, but I pulled down nearly $20,000 in that first year, which was really big money back then.

By the end of the school year I was the second-largest depositor in the bank, after Williams College itself. Over the next three years the "club" was sending 300 students a year to Europe over the summer months and more than 600 students a year to Bermuda and 300 to Nassau for spring break. Though the anti-establishment era was approaching, I figured out that business could be fun, cool and lucrative all at the same time.

Competing travel agents weren't too happy about our club's success, and they complained to the government that we were abusing our non-profit status. I think they had a point. The Civil Aeronautics Board agreed and summoned us to an investigative hearing. I'd had enough of that, so after three years of operation, I retired from the "club." But by then I'd been bitten by the business bug.

Though a history major at Williams, I had an inkling that some type of business career was in my future. That first-hand experience in running a successful business venture would later help me get accepted to Stanford's Graduate School of Business and prepare me for a career in banking. So thank you, Jeffrey Feinstein (and those 200 dental hygienists) for helping me find my calling.

Prologue

The year was 1979. All across the world, disco was topping the charts. In Washington, Jimmy Carter's presidency was paralyzed by the Iranian hostage crisis. And in Ohio's capital, an ambitious banker was toiling to transform the number three bank in Columbus into a household name.

John G. McCoy was no ordinary banker. Here was a man who, fifteen years earlier, had managed to convince Bank of America to make his upstart City National Bank & Trust Ohio's exclusive issuer of a groundbreaking product—the consumer credit card. *Way too risky, father's competitors had warned.* And back when bankers were colorless men in dark suits, John G. had the guts to enlist wacky comedienne Phyllis Diller, who chain-smoked and cackled at her own jokes, as the face of City National in TV and print advertising. *Very unbankerlike, his detractors chided.*

At a time when few banks had offices outside of their hometown or county, father was audacious enough to think bigger. He wanted to break the geographic shackles that limited a bank's reach, and he conjured up a new brand to reflect that vision. The unorthodox name he chose for City National—Bank One—did all those things and more. *No name for a bank, his competitors scoffed.*

The formula worked. By the time father turned the reins over to me several years later, Bank One signs were popping up all over Ohio. What came next would be up to me. As a third-generation banker, I had the McCoy family name to live up to. But more than that, I was determined to fulfill all the promise that the Bank One name implied. This is my story, but it starts with my grandfather.

Here's the Deal

PART ONE
A Family Affair

CHAPTER ONE

Oil or Banking

*J*OHN HALL McCOY entered this world fatherless on September 23, 1887. Not quite penniless, but certainly headed in that direction.

His father, John Edwin McCoy, had tragically died a few months before his birth in a train accident, leaving my grandmother, the former Rosa Estelle Hall, pregnant with their first child. While she was fortunate to receive $2,000 in life insurance (equivalent to about $53,000 today), that wasn't going to last her a lifetime.

On December 20, 1890, Rosa married James M. Leedy, a local lumber dealer in Marietta, Ohio. Their daughter, Cora G. Leedy, was born January 12, 1892. The marriage didn't last.

Leedy left town, and Rosa Hall Leedy and two young children moved in with her grandparents, John G. and Maria Hall, at 123 Maple Street. Rosa reverted to her former name, Rosa Estelle McCoy, and, after her grandfather died, she and her grandmother took in boarders to make ends meet. Among the boarders was Wallace Oscar Dunham, an oil driller from New York she would marry a decade later. After Maria Hall died in 1901, Rosa continued running the boarding house alone. Money remained in short supply.

Young John H. kept the McCoy family name despite his mother's two subsequent marriages. He was in the eighth grade in 1903 when he quit school to work at the Peoples Banking and Trust Company of Marietta, telling friends he needed to support his mother and little sister Cora. He was a messenger by day and janitor by night, and, by all accounts, a diligent worker.

These were the family and financial circumstances that would shape the driven businessman that grandfather would become. And I do mean driven. He returned to work after four heart attacks and suffered his fifth and final one—where else, but in the office.

The Appalachian Basin, of which eastern Ohio was a part, was the leading oil-producing region in the United States from oil's discovery in the late 1800s and into the early 20th century. Marietta oilman David A. Bartlett founded Peoples Bank in 1902 primarily to serve the local oil industry. During those boom times, forests of derricks replaced the oaks and hickories covering area hillsides, yet oil operators often found it hard to secure loans. Bartlett was also a founder of Keener Oil & Gas, which grew to have operations in Ohio, West Virginia, Illinois and Oklahoma. He brought John H. into the company.

John H. also became involved with Pure Oil, which began in Pennsylvania but was also drilling in Oklahoma early in the 20th century. Marietta's Beman Dawes, a former congressman and brother of a vice president of the United States (Charles Dawes was second in command to Republican Calvin Coolidge), was an early chairman and president of Pure Oil, which was later rebranded Union 76.

◄ *Previous page:* The children *(standing, L to R)* of Florence and John H. McCoy: John G., Jane Peterson, Mary Caroline Mildren, Dorothy McCoy and Chuck, in 1953.

As a young man, my grandfather had two potential career paths: oil or banking. He was going back and forth—literally—spending two weeks in Marietta and two weeks in Oklahoma.

Family lore says he finally made up his mind after drilling ten consecutive dry wells on one of those Oklahoma trips. "That's it," he said in disgust. "I've got a family to support."

He returned to Ohio and went into the banking business full time. The eleventh and twelfth wells were reputed to have struck oil, helping to spark what would become the great Oklahoma oil rush, a maker of many fortunes.

John H. was a clerk at Peoples when on November 10, 1909, he married Florence Rebecca Buchanan in the brick St. Luke's Episcopal Church on 2nd Street. The building still stands. Florence was the daughter of Emma Robertson Buchanan and druggist Charles Buchanan. Over the next eleven years, John H. moved up the ranks to become teller, cashier, secretary and treasurer while the family grew to five children. My father, John Gardner McCoy, was their first-born son. (John G.'s mother was Buchanan, not Gardner. He is the exception to the naming convention, though the reason has been lost.) Mary Caroline was the oldest, followed by father, Jane, Dorothy and Charles (Chuck).

As the years passed, my grandfather became a trusted member of management. He and President Bartlett, along with Peoples board member George White, an oilman and member of the U. S. House of Representatives, together reviewed each loan sought by farmers, business owners and oilmen.

In failing health in 1922, Bartlett asked the Peoples board to elect John H. president. After 18 years at the bank he became one of the youngest bank presidents in the country at the age of 35. The *United States Investor* called the promotion "a most popular action," praising John H. as being "of the strong aggressive type which ambitious banks are so desirous of having as their executive heads."

He also became president of Keener Oil & Gas, moving up from secretary and treasurer, company records show. He resigned as president December 22, 1929, when Bartlett's sons, David A. Jr. and Dewey (later to become Oklahoma governor), took over. By then Keener was headquartered in Oklahoma.

When he began as bank president, a hole had been dug for the foundation of what would become the five-story Peoples Bank building at the corner of 2nd and Putnam streets in Marietta. In addition to running the bank and Keener, John H. took on the job of overseeing construction and the move from the bank's original home, the St. Clair Building, down Putnam Street. (The St. Clair Building was constructed in 1900 and named for Arthur St. Clair, the first governor of the Northwest Territory.)

During the grand opening of the Peoples Bank and Trust at its new location, October 18, 1924—a Saturday—bankers from New York to Chicago and a crowd of more than 12,000 passed through the high bronze doors to see the travertine limestone and marble interior, according to press accounts. The staff handed out roses and expensive cigars while also carrying out their banking duties.

Peoples was on the second floor of the building, which later enabled John H. and his employees to keep working when the Muskingum and Ohio rivers overflowed and flooded the streets. To thwart robberies, each teller cage was outfitted with a foot pedal wired to an alarm, and pigeon holes kept loaded guns within reach.

John H., who worked so hard that he would occasionally faint from exhaustion, was a demanding boss. Katherine Freese began working at the bank after finishing her junior year in high school. Her father, a trolley mechanic, had been killed in a work accident when she was four and she was helping support her family.

She told Eugene C. Murdock, author of *The Peoples Bank: an Informal History,* that my grandfather called her into his office just before she was to begin her senior year in high school and asked what her plans were. She responded they were uncertain, but she knew her family had no money to send her to college.

"I didn't go to college," John H. told her. "I didn't even finish high school and I'm president of the bank."

Freese took the bait, skipped her senior year and continued working at the bank.

She described John H. as "a tornado. He was very abrupt. I can't say he didn't have any feelings because he loved his kids and family, but when it came to employees, he didn't stop to think they had feelings, too. Of course, he was a successful banker but many a time I would like to have shaken him." There's more.

He was all business, Freese told Murdock: "At the end of the day, I could not leave when the others left. I was the switchboard (operator) and had to stay there—even after we closed—until Mr. McCoy left. Many a night I would sit there and just watch—there was nothing to do—until eight o'clock. He'd never come back and say goodnight; he'd just get his coat and go out. Then I knew I could leave."

When the bank had closed in the afternoon and John H. was away, the staff would relax and sometimes sing as they finished their work. But never when my grandfather was there, Freese said.

I cringe reading that account. Yes, times were different then and the boss was definitely the boss, but certainly not a management style to emulate today, or one that I would have been comfortable with.

Not surprisingly, John H. put my father to work as an elevator operator in 1926. "My father began teaching us at an early age that we were expected to take a strong interest in working," John G. told *Ohio Business Magazine* reporter Matthew Hall.

That career was quickly halted when a state inspector reminded bank officials they could not employ thirteen-year-olds. I would have loved to see the expression on my grandfather's face when he got that news—from a safe distance, of course!

My uncle, Charles "Chuck" McCoy, the youngest of the five children, told a journalist that his father's absence from home was the norm, and apparently acceptable to my grandmother, Florence. "You had to understand the pact between my mother and father," he said. "She would raise five children and he would work. And that's all he did, all the time."

During the Roaring Twenties, the bank's assets grew steadily and John H. developed friendships with board member White and area business leaders. He became a director of Pure Oil and of a local ice company, and he joined fraternal organizations including the Freemasons and Shriners.

The wild economic growth of the decade came to an abrupt halt with the stock market crash on October 29, 1929, also called Black Tuesday. More than 600 U.S. banks closed that year. Many tried to find buyers; others merged, as Columbus-based Commercial National Bank and City National Bank of Commerce did the day of the crash. They formed City National Bank & Trust—precursor to Bank One—in an effort to survive in the harsh climate, in a market dominated by larger institutions.

Remarkably, as the Great Depression took hold, my grandfather not only kept Peoples Bank solvent, he watched it grow. He was tagged with the nickname "Five Percent McCoy," because while other banks were lowering interest rates to generate loans he insisted people pay full-freight to borrow, and maintained the 5 percent loan rate.

He was elected president of the Marietta Chamber of Commerce in 1930. His friend, White, a Democrat, was elected governor of Ohio that November and took office the following January. With banks in continued crisis, Gov. White asked John H. to serve as a special financial advisor.

By 1932, an additional 5,100 banks had closed nationwide. Congress authorized creation of the Reconstruction Finance Corporation, which would make loans to banks and businesses in trouble. The first RFC president was Marietta's Charles G. Dawes, Beman's brother, a longtime friend of John H. and the former vice president under Calvin Coolidge. Dawes assigned John H. to the Reconstruction Finance Advisory Board.

In this job, John H. learned the troubles of large and small banks throughout the state and provided advice on lending to them. My father told a reporter how John H. would climb into his Packard and "drive fast to Columbus, Cleveland and Washington D.C., sometimes twice a week." There weren't many cars on the road and very few traffic signals back then.

In November 1932, Franklin Delano Roosevelt was elected president in a landslide over incumbent Herbert Hoover. Nearly one-quarter of America's workers could find no jobs and faith in the country's financial institutions plummeted. Banks were closing at a never-before-seen rate as depositors lined up to get their money before their banks shuttered, withdrawing millions of dollars and further weakening the financial system.

Candidate Roosevelt and even Hoover's fellow Republicans had urged him to take aggressive action on the banking crisis and economy, but Hoover refused. In February and March of 1933, Louisiana, New York, California and Michigan declared statewide bank holidays to try to stem the bleeding. Ohio and dozens more states took less drastic steps, authorizing banks to limit transactions.

After a March 2 meeting of bankers and business leaders at the Marietta chamber, members sent Ohio senators Simeon Fess and Robert Bulkley, and Senate Banking Committee Chairman Carter Glass, messages urging immediate help.

According to Murdock's informal history of the bank, John H. told those gathered, "It is of no use to kid yourselves. If you don't get action from Washington, there won't be a factory or store in operation in two weeks' time. It is beyond us as individuals and it is going to get so bad that Washington will have to act. For that reason, the sooner the pressure can be put on the national leaders…the better."

Action came swiftly with the new president. On March 5, 1933, a Sunday and the day after his inauguration, Roosevelt went on the radio and addressed the nation in the first of many fireside chats. He declared a week-long national bank "holiday" would begin the next day, in response to the emergency created by the rapid withdrawals of gold and cash.

That week, Congress debated just forty minutes before adopting the Emergency Banking Act that enabled the federal government to reopen solvent banks and assist those that were salvageable. Slightly more than half were considered fit to reopen and 5 percent—about 1,000—had to be closed. The rest of the U.S. banks were given limits on the amounts that could be withdrawn or allowed only to accept deposits.

In his radio address following the holiday, Roosevelt told sixty million listeners that the crisis was over and the banks were secure. The next day, deposits exceeded withdrawals and by April, $1 billion was deposited back into the banks.

Near Marietta, the First State Bank of Belpre and the First National Bank of Lowell could not meet the federal requirements needed to reopen. John H. oversaw Peoples' purchase of the two banks that spring and made the former presidents managers of their respective banks. As an outgrowth of the banking crisis, the Ohio Legislature created the State Banking Advisory Board in 1933. My grandfather served a three-year term. He was elected vice president of the Ohio Banker's Association in 1934, after serving as chairman of his region.

As a calm hand in the storm, John H. became well known and trusted in banking circles. He knew virtually every bank president and board member in Ohio and through his travels and oversight duties had a good feel for the financial health of institutions across the state. If ever a situation called for a workaholic banker, the Great Depression was it. He was a strong leader and the right man for those times.

In the winter of 1935, the nation's newspapers were overflowing with coverage of the "Crime of the Century"—the kidnapping and murder of the young son of aviation hero Charles Lindbergh. Begrudgingly, perhaps, newspapers in both Marietta and Columbus found room for this blurb: City National Bank, an RFC borrower in Columbus, had named John H. McCoy president. Most likely the news was greeted with a collective shrug. Grandfather always said he took the job because it was a bigger bank in a more cosmopolitan city.

The deal had been made after Gov. White lost his re-election bid that November and made plans to return home to Marietta. Ira J. Fulton, the state superintendent of banks whom John H. had befriended while working on the state advisory board, would become president of Peoples.

Peoples' assets had grown from $4 million in 1920 to $8 million by the time John H. left. City National had slightly more than $18 million in deposits but was a distant third in the Columbus market.

The Huntingtons, with Huntington Bank, and the Wolfes, with Ohio National Bank (later to be called BancOhio), dominated Columbus banking. Ohio National had the bulk of commercial lending and was, by far, the largest bank in town, while Huntington was strong in the trust business. The two banks controlled nearly all the correspondent business (correspondent banks conduct business on behalf of other banks and generate reliable and low-risk income from those services). City National was a financial sapling struggling to grow in the shade of two towering oaks.

Grandfather was not deterred by his bank's junior status. I'm sure he assessed the situation and quickly determined that outworking the competition was as good a place as any to start. He needed to impose his brand of discipline and harden City National's beleaguered troops for battle. One of his first initiatives was to ban coffee in bank offices and forbid alcohol at lunch. You can imagine a bunch of senior loan officers congregating at the bulletin board and dousing cigarettes in half empty cups of coffee after reading that office memo! Who does this McCoy think he is, they must have grumbled, or words to that effect.

But that was just an opening salvo. City National needed an entirely new approach to emerge from the shadows of the major banks, and grandfather had an idea. He had seen, on his RFC rounds, that small installment-loan companies weren't failing at the rate banks were. Why? Because all the risk was spread over many small loans, as opposed to several major commercial borrowers. He decided that City National's best chance for success was to focus on something that Ohio National, Huntington and most other financial institutions had largely ignored: retail banking.

It was unorthodox and a gamble on many levels. Yet it proved to be an innovative idea that propelled City National into the banking big leagues and influenced an entire industry.

CHAPTER TWO

California Gleaning

*I*n 1936, John G. McCoy was a Marietta College graduate who had just finished his first year of business school at Harvard. While visiting relatives in California with his mother and sisters, grandfather sent father a note suggesting he visit Stanford Business School. John G. complied, and wrote a note back that he'd had "an interesting day" at Stanford.

Grandfather wasn't satisfied. He picked up the phone and called father.

"You didn't get the message," grandfather said.

"What do you mean?" father replied.

"I want you to go there."

Father was perplexed. He told John H. that he was quite comfortable at Harvard, had a nice roommate and had already bought his books for the upcoming session.

"I don't know anything about that," John H. said, "but I do know they're doing things differently on the West Coast."

John G. continued to make his case for Harvard. Grandfather listened, but finally told him, "John, that's fine with me. But if you want to join me at the bank, you either finish at Stanford, or stay at Harvard and then go to California and work for two years."

Grandfather prevailed. His son transferred to Stanford and, as instructed, studied what Bank of America founder Amadeo Peter "A.P." Giannini was doing with consumer banking.

At the turn of the 20th century, banking was for the wealthy. Giannini was the son of struggling Italian immigrants who had been refused accounts by traditional banks. After becoming a prosperous grocery wholesaler, he founded the Bank of Italy in San Francisco in 1904 and was an innovator from the start. He made loans to immigrants, farmers, small businesses, women and minorities. The bank's loans and deposits quintupled within a year.

An early claim to fame came in the days after the devastating San Francisco earthquake of 1906, which sparked fires that crippled the city. Giannini moved the vault's money to his home outside the fire zone in rural San Mateo, in a horse-drawn garbage wagon to protect against theft. While fires kept other banks from opening their vaults for weeks, Giannini was one of the few who was able to provide loans. He actually ran his bank from a plank across two barrels out on the docks, making handshake loans and distributing cash. Now that's a banker who wasn't afraid to be close to the customer!

In 1909, Giannini began purchasing banks throughout California, converting them into branches of the Bank of Italy. By 1918 the Bank of Italy had become the first statewide bank in the United States. The name was

◄ *Previous page:* The Columbus Club was the venue for this dinner honoring my grandfather John H. McCoy *(seated at head of table with vest)*, who ran City National Bank from 1935 until his death in 1958. At the far left *(forefront)* is my maternal grandfather Frank Bonnet, a bank director, with my Uncle Chuck McCoy across from him *(far right)*. John G. McCoy is standing, third from the right.

changed to Bank of America in 1930, and shortly after it would become the largest banking institution in the world.

BofA was rewriting the banking playbook, and father was there to witness it first-hand. And in business, imitation is the sincerest form of flattery. After graduating from Stanford, John G. returned to Columbus in 1937 to work with grandfather, beginning what would be a long and fruitful career in Ohio banking. That same year, City National followed BofA's lead and began to offer customers installment loans, one of the first banks outside of California to do so.

A funny aside about father and Stanford. When John G. celebrated his fiftieth year in banking, the bank honored him with an endowed chair in his name at the university's Graduate School of Business. We told father to figure out how it should be named and in what subject.

John G. loved details, so he flew out to California to meet with the dean, who also headed up the accounting department. The dean matter-of-factly told father that Stanford only had availability for chairs in accounting, and not in any other field. Father was chagrined. "I'm not all that interested in accounting," John G. said.

Then father pulled one of his classic moves. "You might not be aware of it," he began, "but I went to Harvard for a year before coming to Stanford. Maybe I should go check with them and see what they have available."

Say no more. Dad got his chair and a suitable name to go with it—the John G. McCoy-Bank One Corporation Professorship of Creativity and Innovation at Stanford. It sure looks great on a business card.

On January 4, 1941, my father married Jeanne Bonnet, the eldest of three daughters of Frank and Florence (Newlove) Bonnet. My grandparents Frank and Florence were college sweethearts and both graduates of The Ohio State University Class of 1909. The Bonnets were Huguenots, or French Protestants, who faced discrimination in France. The Bonnets at some point emigrated to Germany and then to the United States. It was said that grandfather Bonnet spoke German as a child before English, though he was born in the United States.

Frank Bonnet worked for Buckeye Steel Castings in Columbus, an iron foundry and railcar manufacturer that in the early 20th century was run by Samuel Prescott Bush, who was the grandfather of U.S. President George H. W. Bush and great grandfather of President George W. Bush. Bonnet family lore holds that S.P. Bush was a real taskmaster. Grandfather Bonnet ended up as president, chairman of the board and major stockholder of the company that was established in 1881. John H. McCoy also served on the company's board of directors, as did father after grandfather died.

Not even a year after father and Jeanne Bonnet were married, Japan bombed Pearl Harbor on Dec. 7, 1941. The very next day the United States declared war on Japan and entered into World War II. Father joined the Navy and grandfather took on yet another role: area chairman of war bond sales.

I came along June 11, 1943, followed three and a half years later by the birth of my sister and only sibling, Virginia. (Everyone calls her Jinny, and she calls me Dede, because she couldn't pronounce Johnny when she was a child.) My father was on active duty when I was born and didn't see me for a whole year. More on that later.

Things were relatively quiet on the home front as the war progressed, but in 1943, grandfather suffered his first heart attack. With my father in the service and grandfather limited to bed rest, the family turned to my Uncle Chuck. Seven years my father's junior, Chuck McCoy had also graduated from Marietta College and Stanford Business School, where he wrote a graduate dissertation on the oil business. He had stayed out West and joined Standard Oil of California after graduation.

A tearful grandmother Florence called Chuck and asked him to return to Ohio to help run the bank. He agreed without much hesitation, though I'm sure he agonized privately over the decision. Chuck was stateside because although he had been a football, basketball and tennis captain at Marietta College, he had a heart irregularity that doctors detected when he tried to enlist in the military.

Chuck was a little green to be running things but certainly had the intellect and educational background to fill the breach. He also had plenty of coaching from the sidelines—or in this case, from the bedside.

"Back then, if you had a heart attack, you had to lie in bed for five months," Chuck told a journalist. "My job was to be grilled every night by my father about what went on at the bank. As a result, I learned banking and he had something to look forward to."

When he did return to work, John H. wasn't permitted to drive for several weeks. Aunt Dorothy McCoy, my father's sister, was given the job of shuttling grandfather to and from work from his home on Ashbourne Road in Bexley.

"We're going to make it all the way with no red lights," she would promise him. By all accounts Dorothy did a fine job timing traffic signals as they traveled three miles west on Broad Street to the bank, which sat across from the Ohio Statehouse.

After John H. recuperated, the Federal Reserve Board in Cleveland named him in 1944 to the Federal Advisory Council, one of twelve individuals from across the U.S. to consult and advise the Board of Governors of the Federal Reserve. It was a great honor to be selected and subsequently both my father and I had the same opportunity with the advisory council.

On June 6, 1944, the war took a favorable turn for the U.S. and its allies with the successful D-Day landings at Normandy, France. Father was extremely close to the action, serving on a Navy supply ship that arrived in the Normandy theater three days after the initial assault. The situation remained perilous with German U-boats prowling the seas and sinking dozens of ships.

Almost seven months earlier, having twice seen his first-born, and not sure whether he would return home alive or become a casualty of war, father sat down and wrote me, on U.S. Navy stationary, a touching letter in neat cursive script that was intended to be read by me in the event of his death. (Mother finally gave it to me when I left for college.) I've kept it all these years, and it continues to mean a lot to me:

Sunday afternoon
September 19th 1943
My dear Son:

This is the first letter I have written to you, and I want you to know a few things that are on my mind.

Today you are to be christened. Therefore it is an important day for you and also for your parents. As you grow older you alone will learn the importance of believing in God. You also will be given the opportunity to have your own religion. Whatever you do, you must always keep faith in the Lord.

You, I think, are very fortunate, as I was. You have a really most wonderful mother. Sometimes you may disagree with her but always remember, and please take my word for it, that she will always place your interest before hers. And son, that should mean everything to you.

Your grand-parents are all wonderful. They too will do many unnecessary things for you. Learn to be appreciative, thankful and respectful to them all.

At the present time, I'm aboard a ship soon to go to sea. And while I have only seen you two different times I feel as though I were living with you every hour. Your Mother and I have long looked forward to the day you would arrive and you are more to us than anything else that exist (sic). Because of this, you have assumed an obligation. If by the wish of the Lord I'm not to return, you then, will have many more obligations. I think I may be able to sum them all up in two points.

First, is the one to your Mother, and now, you will be all she has in this world. You must therefore try to provide for her, what I might have been able to do. I know you will never be selfish, but sometimes it may be hard to think of her before thinking of yourself. But truly what I know is, what you will do, and that is the way I hope it will be. Knowing your Mother as I do, she will always think of you before she does herself. All that I can ask is for you to love her and have as much respect and devotion as I do for her.

Second, there is yourself to think about. Above all be honest and truthful. Be happy and enjoy life, and son you will only get out of life a portion of what you put into it. Therefore in everything you do, no matter how big or small, put into it everything you have, and in the years to come you will in many ways be repaid. But if you try to obtain from life more than you give, then without doubt, you will become a failure, and your entire existence will fail in its purpose.

With the highest hopes and desires for your success in life, and for your and your Mother's happiness, I'm with all my love, Your Dad.

It's easy to imagine a homesick serviceman pondering his fate in the dark hours of World War II. He never said much about the war, and a comment he made to me years later, when Jane and I were preparing for a visit to Normandy marking the 60th anniversary of the invasion, was telling. I asked father to tell me what Normandy was like. "I have no interest in discussing it with you," he said. That was it. I did not press him. When he said no, it meant no, and I got the message. I think he saw a lot of death and destruction, and needless to say, the war years were not among father's fondest memories.

Victory was declared in Europe on May 8, 1945, and with Japan three months later. Father and millions of military personnel returned home. Soon, the U.S. economy was growing again. Consumer spending replaced the penny-pinching of the Depression and war years. Along with a baby boom, the post-war years were marked with the growth of the suburbs: single-family homes with appliances, garages and cars. Grandfather, who now had two sons to help and advise him, had positioned City National to take advantage of the burgeoning retail market.

John H. was consumed by the banking business and numerous service roles. When it came to family, however, he was very much on the periphery.

Of course I was just a boy when he was alive, so my recollections are clouded with the fog of time and childhood. One image remains: I really don't ever remember him *not* having a tie on. He carried himself as the patriarch, a regulator and a banker. You never really saw a softer side, the kind of affable grandfather you might read about or see in a movie.

My sister Jinny and cousin Bill Mildren would sometimes sheepishly visit his home office, and recall being fascinated with a cast-iron bank—a hunter firing a gun—that sat on a bookshelf. But we all knew to keep our distance. "He was a businessman, working since the eighth grade, and he simply didn't know how to be around kids," is how Jinny puts it. "He scared the daylights out of me." I think she was on the mark.

Our grandmother Florence, on the other hand, was everything you wanted a grandmother to be. In Jinny's words she was, "the sweetest woman in the world."

One time grandmother went on a cruise with a friend, and she asked my Aunt Ruth, who was married to Uncle Chuck, to make grandfather breakfast every day before he left for work. Most people can make their own breakfast, so I asked her what that was like.

"He ate the same meal every morning," Ruth recalled. "He had to have a perfectly cooked soft-boiled egg—not too hard, not too soft."

John H. was opinionated and tough, with a short temper, she said. "But he was very nice and thanked me for breakfast each morning. Dad McCoy was always kind to me, but I never ceased being afraid that I might make the wrong move and upset him."

During the next dozen years, grandfather suffered three more heart attacks, but kept on as City National president. Directors and officers of the bank held a dinner at a private club in Columbus in December 1953, honoring his fifty years in the industry. Franklin O. Schoedinger, a longtime director of City National, presented grandfather with a silver tray.

Other honors piled up. He was a member and president of the Columbus Country Club, a member of the Columbus Club, the Ohio State University Club and Faculty Club, the Shrine, Knights Templar and Scottish Rite and the Broad Street Presbyterian Church. He served on the finance and investment committee of the OSU Board of Trustees. He was a trustee at Marietta College, chairman of the board of Buckeye Steel Castings Co., and a director of the Capital City Products Co.

Frail at seventy-one, he was still running the bank when he suffered his fifth and fatal attack. He died at White Cross Hospital on November 18, 1958.

His pallbearers and honorary pall bearers included leaders of OSU and Marietta College, bank and business moguls, a U.S. senator and more.

My sister Jinny summed it up best: "He may have worked himself to death, but I think it's what he enjoyed."

This much is certain: Bank One (the successor bank to City National) almost certainly would not have become the consumer banking powerhouse that it was without the foundation laid by John H. McCoy. Grandfather lost his childhood, sacrificed his family life and compromised his health for the good of the bank. His manner may have been rough by today's standards, but his legacy as a banker, regulator and civic leader will endure. The McCoy family, the state of Ohio and dare I say current JPMorgan Chase shareholders all owe him a debt of gratitude.

CHAPTER THREE

Dignity or Dividends

After grandfather died in 1958, John G. was named president of City National, serving under CEO Walter R. Reiter, who sadly died of cancer nine months later. Father was forty-four years old, considered very young to be a bank president at that time. Chuck McCoy, who had been vice president since 1952, became a director at the tender age of thirty-seven.

In those days, the brothers were more competitive than close. They each had their own circle of friends, though they would occasionally play bridge together with their wives. Chuck yearned for greater independence after playing second fiddle to a dominating father and older brother for so many years.

He had been approached by other banks and interviewed for several positions while his father was alive, but he never pulled the trigger. In one magazine article, Chuck said he'd tried several times to leave, "but my father always put the kibosh on that."

According to his wife, Ruth, "After his father died, Chuck felt he could leave. We felt awful about leaving Mother McCoy, but Chuck just had to get out of the bank because John Gardener McCoy was coming back and he said he was darned if he was going to work for him." They didn't tell any of the McCoys about the plans they were formulating.

As was customary for executives looking to jump ship in those pre-internet days, Chuck put an anonymous ad for his services in *The American Banker*, listing his qualifications and a post office box where banks could contact him.

The first response he received was from John G., inviting him for an interview! "We had more fun with that," Ruth recalled. "Chuck said, 'I'm just tempted to accept the invitation and go to the interview, and let him find out that way.'"

But Chuck didn't give in to the temptation. He quietly found a new position, told his family he'd accepted a job at Louisiana National Bank in Baton Rouge, and moved south. Two years later he became the bank's president. Meanwhile, at City National in Columbus, the John G. era had begun.

Shortly after grandfather died, father went to Jamaica for a short getaway, where he had time to ponder what he wanted to do. Here's what he had inherited from his father: the 258th largest bank in the United States, the thirty-eighth largest bank in Ohio and the third largest bank in Columbus—and there were only three banks in Columbus at the time. In the 1950s, Ohio's capital city was very much a sleepy college town, nothing like the economically diverse and dynamic boom-town it has become.

So this was not a very big thing that he had, and he had to figure out how he wanted to compete with the leading banks in town. This much he

◄ *Previous page:* Wacky comedienne Phyllis Diller was the unorthodox spokesperson for plucky City National Bank in the 1960s.

Here's the Deal

knew: "Right away I realized that I wanted to run a Tiffany's and not a Woolworth's," he told *The New York Times* in 1981.

In 1958, Ohio National Bank was the largest of the Columbus banks, counting as customers nearly all of the major corporations, public institutions and family businesses of any importance. Huntington National Bank, founded in 1866, was the second largest and dominated the trust business. Both of these banks had long-standing relationships with customers that had survived depressions, recessions, wars and other hard times.

Father understood that he wasn't going to get the business from the electric company or the leading wealthy families in town. He had to find a different business to go after, and that's what ultimately led him to the retail customer and small-business person. While it sounds like an obvious conclusion to draw today, at the time it was quite novel.

People don't remember this, but well into the 1970s, many Americans got paid in cash. You'd get a little envelope with your money, and working people didn't come into the bank very often because the industry wasn't so customer friendly back then.

My father understood that the consumer society was growing, and he smartly figured out that the retail side of banking would be the business to be in. City National was the only bank in town offering consumers small installment loans as the centerpiece of a more personalized banking experience. As far as the little guy was concerned, they certainly lived up to this advertising slogan: "The loaningest bank in town."

Part and parcel of doing business with the masses was making the bank itself a nicer place to visit. When grandfather ran the bank, there were bars to keep people out. City National branches were the first in town to replace intimidating teller cages with more inviting open-air counters. New branches had carpeting and modern lighting, in addition to community rooms and kitchen facilities for hosting neighborhood meetings.

A *Columbus Dispatch* reporter called a new City National branch "friendly" and "one of the finest structures of its kind."

Father was an early advocate of research and development, a notion more associated with science and industry than banking. John G. wanted to spend up to three percent of profits on new things. Some of them worked out, and some didn't. A pre-computer era version of electronic "home banking" requiring couplers attached to whizzing and whirring telephone handsets was a spectacular flop—but only because the technology of the day couldn't support what was obviously a brilliant idea.

But even in failure you'd learn why you failed, which allowed you to move ahead. One reason we were among the first to jump into internet banking in a big way is because we always had our fingers in these sorts of things. You might say we were hard-wired to try new things.

When innovations worked, they generally went gangbusters. One such great idea was drive-up banking. Sure, other banks had experimented with drive-up windows through the years, in some cases knocking a hole in the wall and installing a sliding window that could be difficult to pull up to. But nothing had been built from the ground up.

That changed in June 1955, when City National opened its first drive-through banking branch, according to some histories the first in the nation designed specifically for that purpose. (Grandfather was still in charge then, but father and Uncle Chuck had considerable influence and were behind some of those 1950s innovations.)

The branch, at 3100 W. Broad Street, was specially designed by Chuck for drive-through business and aimed at upwardly mobile suburban customers. The branch had clearly marked lanes leading to four windows and promised sixty-second in-and-out transactions. It was so groundbreaking that Bank of America came out to see it. That was some compliment, because Giannini's BofA was at the forefront of the consumer banking revolution.

Because father was much younger than the typical bank president (the title CEO was rarely used in the 1950s), he and the board thought he needed an experienced banker in senior management for introductions, advice and counsel. After his caretaker CEO passed away less than a year into father's tenure, the search resumed for a "gray-haired" banker with industry and community connections to join the management team.

Father found his man in Everett D. Reese, a nationally recognized banker and just the person that he needed. In 1921, Ohio-raised and educated Reese was an economics teacher at Georgia Tech who was being recruited by Park National Bank, the smallest of five banks in Newark, Ohio, by men to whom he had sold bonds some years earlier while in college. He left academia and started working as a teller at Park. His superiors must have been impressed, because in 1927 Park made him the youngest bank president in the country, just shy of his thirtieth birthday. A decade later, Park National was bigger than all its competitors combined.

Reese was active in state and national banking organizations, and in 1953, when he was fifty-five, was elected president of the American Bankers Association. He hired John Alford to replace him at Park during the one-year-term, which required him to travel all across the country, but also wisely invested in two other financial institutions before he took up the national post—one being State Savings Bank in Columbus. Reese didn't know what the future held for him after his ABA stint, so he was hedging his bets with the investments in case he needed a place to work. He rightly suspected that Park wouldn't be big enough for him and Alford.

Reese owned State Savings and was back at Park when father hired him in 1960. Reese was by no means a banking innovator, but he had the stature that father lacked and valuable industry and political connections in Ohio and nationally that would open doors for City National.

Father had a business philosophy that I admired—one that I tried to emulate when I ran the bank—and it served him well. He tried to hire above himself and wasn't afraid to pay people accordingly.

"Don't be afraid to pay a talented person more money than you're making," he'd say. "Hire the best people and then delegate. There's no use putting someone in who is the best in the world and then telling that person how to do things."

He loved to say that if you hire smart people, they'll make you look smart, and if you hire dumb people, you'll end up looking dumb. Ev Reese was one of those smart people, and bringing him on board made father look even smarter.

In those early years, I'm sure a lot of people thought Chairman Ev Reese was running City National. That was always the thing about father—he didn't really care about titles, but he recognized their importance to others. He knew he was running the bank, and Ev Reese knew who was running the bank, and John G. didn't care whether the man on the street knew he was running the bank. That's just how father was.

In a 1998 interview, father told *Columbus Monthly* magazine that he wasn't concerned about being overshadowed by a towering figure like Reese.

"I was succeeding my father, and I thought Ev had a wonderful reputation," he said. "If I could get Ev to come and help me, it would help me bridge the gap between myself and my father's career."

It was through Reese that father was introduced to another very smart person who wasn't a banker, but was very instrumental in City National's growth and success. He even came up with the game-changing "Bank One" name that we introduced in 1979.

John Fisher was an advertising and communications professional who had a degree in radio journalism from Ohio State and was breaking into the business as a disc jockey at radio station WCLT-AM in Newark, a small town thirty-five miles east of Columbus. He wore lots of hats at the station including spinning the hits of the day; writing and reading news items and helping local advertisers create their on-air copy. The latter skill was what appealed to father.

Fisher's trademark at the station was his uncanny ability to predict the weather long before satellites and radar turned forecasting into a fairly predictable science.

His secret? The DJ had a friend who lived near Port Columbus International Airport—about twenty-five miles west of the radio station—who would call in whenever it started raining. That gave Fisher just enough time to break into programming and let listeners know it was time to bring in the laundry or roll up the car windows. People loved it and he looked like a genius.

Father knew that if he was going after the retail customer, he needed advertising. No doubt Reese played up Fisher's advertising credentials and creative abilities (possibly with his fingers crossed), because if he had told father that they ought to go hire this funny radio DJ who can predict thunderstorms, father might have blown his stack.

Always willing to take a chance on a bright person, John G. put Fisher in charge of his newly created advertising department at a time when television was emerging as the dominant form of media in the country. John G. didn't mind that Fisher wasn't a banker—he had plenty of those at his disposal. Father wanted Fisher to figure out what customers wanted, and Fisher delivered time and again. The common theme was convenience.

Among Fisher's hires was Ron Castell, a marketing executive from the Columbus department store chain Lazarus to help connect with retail customers. In keeping with the late-'60s style, he had long hair and a big moustache, more akin to Cheech and Chong than Currier and Ives.

When a local business reporter questioned John G. about Castell's hippie appearance, father replied, "I care more about what's in his head than what's on his head."

Above all else, City National needed to stand out from the crowd. Fisher's advertising department went way out on a limb by hiring comedienne Phyllis Diller as City National's spokesperson in 1962. Diller was a wise-cracking Ohio native with wildly teased blond hair who wore outrageous outfits and cackled at her own jokes, which frequently belittled her uninspired husband "Fang." Diller was a staple of late-night television variety shows and arguably the least likely bank pitch person in America. (For younger readers, Diller, who died in 2012 at the age of ninety-five, lent her voice to the Ant Queen character in the animated film, *A Bug's Life*.)

In one commercial, Diller discovers the marvels of drive-through banking, but not before she pulls up to the banking window and attempts to order a cheeseburger and fries. In another, she says that City National "even made a loan to my husband Fang," but "of course he put me up for collateral."

Diller even has some fun with Father in a third commercial. "I just met the president of City National Bank!" she proclaims. "I walked into his office and said, 'I'm the president of the Good Neighbor Fan Club.' He smiled and I kissed his hand. Oh, I love him! Look, want to do your banking at a friendly bank? Switch over to City National. I buy all my clothes there!"

The spots were so different from what other banks were doing at the time, and really helped to put City National on the map. "For any bank to hire a free spirit like Phyllis Diller to be your spokesperson in the early 1960s, especially a small bank in Columbus, Ohio, it just shows you how willing they were to take chances," said my first cousin on the Bonnet side, Jay Hoster, whose mother Anne and my mother were sisters. "Because they were the third bank in Columbus, they had to try something." (In later years, as a Christmas gift for my father, Jay got Diller to sign the jacket of one of her books, "To John G., my favorite banker." Father loved that.)

What today we might call *guerilla marketing* was simply a shocking departure from tradition back then. While other banks were doing institutional advertising ("We're solid, we're strong"), City National was coming right out and saying, "We want to loan you money." A bank with a wacky female comedian spokesperson? The GEICO gecko had nothing on Phyllis Diller, let me tell you!

Some board members were concerned that the irreverent comic did not convey the dignified image typically associated with banks, and they made those feelings known at board meetings. Fisher told *Institutional Investor* in 1991 that father defended the offbeat approach by saying, "'Gentlemen, it's very simple: You can have either dignity or dividends. I vote for dividends.'"

As head of marketing and public relations, Fisher succeeded in creating a can-do image for City National with clever slogans including "The loaningest bank in town" and "The best all-around bank all around town." A magazine-style brochure from 1965 introducing the bank's new downtown headquarters and office building, no doubt written by Fisher, describes the new structure as "warm and friendly as a firm handshake" and boasts that it will deliver "more and better banking for more and more people." (A diagram of the third floor shows the Advertising Department occupying a spacious corner office, just above the executive offices, if that is any indication of what father thought of his creative DJ adman!)

Fisher's unconventional ideas were not limited to advertising. He was an innovator at heart who embraced technology as a means of bringing convenience to customers. The result was a series of innovations—from credit cards to ATMs and debit cards—that helped City National leapfrog not just its cross-town competitors, but most of the banking industry.

Dignity or no dignity, by the mid-1960s City National was gaining a higher profile among competitors and customers. And, by the way, the dividends were pretty good, too.

CHAPTER FOUR

Age of Innovation

*I*n 1958, the same year father started as president, Bank of America introduced BankAmericard (later rebranded as Visa), the first consumer credit card program available to middle-class Americans and smaller merchants. BofA started issuing the cards in Fresno, California, with plans to offer them throughout the state.

Originally made of paper, the early credit cards had the name of the holder on the front with the bank's phone number on the back. Merchants had to be enlisted to accept the card, and participating stores would call the bank for authorization if the purchase price was more than a small fixed amount, say twenty-five or fifty dollars, printed on the front. Once approved, the bank guaranteed payment to the merchant, and collected a fee of between one percent and five percent in the process.

This was really something new. Department stores and oil companies had been issuing similar cards to customers for use in their stores or service stations, but banks offering a general-purpose card that could be used at a variety of merchants? It was very much an alien concept.

Father was aware of the BofA experiment and quickly decided that credit cards would be a natural extension of City National's consumer focus. Banks in Pittsburgh and Indianapolis were developing similar cards for use in those cities, and John G. worried that if an out-of-town bank came into his market with a successful program, he could be squashed.

In 1963, he dispatched Reese and Fisher to California to make the case for City National being awarded the Ohio franchise for BankAmericard. The Californians curtly replied that City National was too small, thank you very much, and sent the Columbus delegation home empty-handed.

But not for long. BofA was indeed interested in expanding its credit-card program. In 1965, BofA started to offer licensing agreements with a collection of banks, and, despite its small size, selected City National for the Ohio franchise in 1966, one of only twelve outside of California. This was a major coup, and perhaps more than anything set the stage for City National's continued growth. Who would have ever thought that we would eventually become the largest credit card issuer in the world.

What made BofA change its mind about City National? When I look back, I imagine the California folks viewed us as an innovative and retail-oriented bank at a time when the largest banks in Ohio—Cleveland's AmeriTrust or Cincinnati's Fifth Third, to take two examples—were not. And it didn't hurt that we had proactively inquired about the franchise years before.

◄ *Previous page:* When City National became the first bank in America to install cash-dispensing machines in all its branches, they looked something like this early model. Innovations including ATMs, credit cards and drive through branches were instrumental in the rise of City National and later Bank One.

City National could have attempted to create its own credit card network by enlisting Columbus merchants, but the card wouldn't have been any good in other communities and of limited value. The BankAmericard network, which included national retailers in addition to local ones, had far greater potential as it was already recognized and increasingly trusted.

Still, BankAmericard was no plug-and-play franchise. City National and other banks in the network had to sign up merchants in their markets to accept the cards, a process that would take years. Many were reluctant to pay the fee required for a sale. We mass-mailed cards to potential users, starting with bank customers and organizations including the Junior League and various country clubs.

Here's how a transaction worked in the 1960s: A shopper, who didn't have to be a City National account holder, would present the card. The merchant would call the bank, and a credit card employee, after referring to a printed list of cardholders and their credit limits, would decide whether to approve the transaction. At one point we had dozens of employees fielding phone calls on the twentieth floor of the bank's 100 E. Broad St. headquarters, flipping through pages of cardholder accounts. Point-of-sale card readers and computers would eventually streamline the process, putting us at the forefront of these revolutionary changes.

As credit cards gained consumer and merchant acceptance, more banks wanted to get in the game. A couple of years after BankAmericard's national rollout, rival banks formed the InterBank Card Association and issued MasterCharge cards, now known as MasterCard Worldwide. The rise of MasterCard was actually good for BankAmericard, as it only widened the acceptance and expanded the market for all credit cards.

Other Ohio banks—including AmeriTrust and Fifth Third—came to City National for help getting started. Because we had the infrastructure in place, we could handle all the authorization and data processing duties for them, leaving the banks to sign up merchants in their markets. This became a separate business for us, processing credit card transactions for other banks.

So by 1968, City National had helped issue more than one million credit cards through fifty banks.

This spunky third-place Columbus bank, with wacky Phyllis Diller and marching bands in commercials, played a significant role in making BankAmericard the first nationally accepted credit card. This innovation not only poured revenue and credibility into City National but helped transform Americans' buying and spending habits, ushering in the "age of plastic." (By 2000, when I left the bank, we had grown into the world's largest issuer of Visa cards, with sixty-five million customers.)

Having that first BankAmericard franchise in Ohio had a side benefit that became more apparent over time. It required City National to elevate its data-processing capabilities beyond what was necessary for a bank its size. Because of that card and the infrastructure needed to support our customers and the other banks issuing credit cards through us, our data processing footprint was a lot bigger than a typical bank. Those capabilities would position us to be first in market with many other innovations.

John Fisher played an increasingly important role at City National as he continued to learn the banking business. Computers were just coming into their own, and he was an early adopter. His willingness to experiment, combined with his great feel for what consumers wanted from a bank, made Fisher a real force in changing the face of banking over the course of his 33-year career. (John Fisher died June 27, 2008, at the age of eighty.)

On Columbus Day 1970, he activated what is generally considered the country's first automated teller machine (ATM) at the Kingsdale Shopping Center branch in Upper Arlington, a suburb of Columbus. At Fisher's urging, City National became the first bank in the country to install ATMs in all of its branches.

The machine's manufacturer was an automated baggage-handling company from Dallas called Docutel, and the man who ran the company was the brother of "Dandy" Don Meredith, a former NFL player and later *Monday Night Football* announcer. A few banks in Europe had experimented with ATMs developed by other manufacturers, but customer acceptance was lukewarm. In Europe, for example, some early models accepted only single-use tokens or vouchers which were retained by the machine. Not nearly as convenient as today's card.

Always on the lookout for something new, Fisher got wind that Docutel was looking for customers for its cash-dispensing machine that promised 24-hour access to money. The funny thing about banking is that nobody wants to be the first to try something new. After one or two banks give something a try, others pay attention but still wait. Then after the third or fourth adopter, everybody wants in and it's a stampede.

Fisher wanted to be first, and sometimes he was first and wrong. But when he was first *and* right, we made lots of money and generally retained our lead when other banks got in. It took a long time for ATMs to catch on for reasons including the impersonal nature of the transaction and fear of mistakes or getting robbed. But once people adapted, the ATM proved to be indispensable for millions of customers and extremely profitable for the bank.

The first generation of ATMs required a dedicated card as the access mechanism. Ours was called the Bank 24 Card, referring to the "always open" nature of the machine itself. As it turned out, customers didn't really want to carry a card with such a narrow focus, but that's how it started. Later on, a customer's Visa card could also be used at our ATMs. And while that was more convenient for most people, customers weren't wild about borrowing money on their credit cards, and potentially paying interest to us, for the privilege of withdrawing cash from their checking accounts.

Fisher wanted to find a way to make our Bank 24 Card more versatile. What if merchants would accept our ATM card just as they would cash or a credit card, he wondered. Then money for purchases would come directly from a customer's checking account, as if there was a virtual City National ATM machine at the checkout counter. If all merchants accepted ATM cards, then cash and credit cards could become a thing of the past. It was an interesting thought.

Fisher convinced a handful of merchants to give it a go. In 1971, Kingsdale served as the venue for what became known as our "cashless society" experiment, with our Bank 24 Card substituting for money. The test involved 28 stores, including the first Limited women's clothing store, which was located at Kingsdale. (Limited Brands founder Leslie Wexner, a Columbus native and Ohio State graduate, was a big fan of my father because dad was the first banker to take a chance on the young innovator who pioneered the specialty retail store concept. Les named his first store "The Limited" because he anticipated having just one, though it grew into an international chain of stores including not only The Limited but also Express, Victoria's Secret and Bath & Body Works.)

So all these Kingsdale stores started to accept our Bank 24 Card as payment. The revolutionary aspect was that the money wasn't borrowed, as with a credit card, but taken directly out of the customer's bank account.

If it sounds suspiciously like today's debit card, that's exactly what it was. But there was no such product at the time. Fisher was among the first people in the world to see the potential of the debit card, something that looked and functioned like a credit card, but unlike a credit card withdrew money from a customer's checking account. We called it a debit card because funds were "debited" from a checking account rather than loaned from a credit-card account.

Visa also recognized the power of Fisher's idea and in 1972 agreed to issue our new debit cards, which could also be used at department stores and gas stations, just like a credit card. That was the beginning of a trend that would dramatically change banking and consumer behavior in years to come, and little City National was once again at the forefront.

But we're getting ahead of ourselves. While it's hard to imagine today, the debit card was not an instant hit. All things being equal, consumers felt they were better off using their credit cards and paying off the balance at the end of the month (no interest would be charged in that case) rather than having funds immediately debited from their checking account. It wasn't until we started charging an annual fee of $50 or $100 for our credit cards that we succeeded in driving significant numbers of customers to the debit card, which we issued for free.

As for the cashless society, well, we're still not there yet. We're certainly a lot closer with widespread use of debit cards and new methods of electronic payment including PayPal and Apple Pay. But I still carry cash in my pocket, and I'll bet you do, too. Fisher was a visionary who saw that something big was about to happen with electronic payments, but it took almost fifty years to come to fruition and we still have a ways to go.

City National eventually pulled the plug on the cashless society experiment at Kingsdale because it never generated the volume of business necessary to make it worthwhile for merchants. Think of it this way: If approximately 20 percent of Kingsdale shoppers were City National customers, and some percentage of them were carrying our Bank 24 Card, that volume wasn't going to be enough for merchants to bother with.

In my time running the bank, Kingsdale would continue to serve as a new products and services laboratory. We introduced a full-service banking facility called a "Financial Marketplace" with supermarket hours—open seventy-two hours a week including Sunday afternoons. The state-of-the-art merchandising system comprised boutiques offering home financing, travel services, business loan operations, a Realtor and investment services.

Colorful neon lights identified each separate service area. Interactive (touch-screen) video displays answered customer questions, and drive-in windows made for quick and easy personal service. Two of our subsidiaries (investment services and travel) and two private companies (Nationwide Insurance and HER Realtors) leased boutique space. Leasing offered us the advantage of learning how to sell products which banks by law could not provide while creating awareness of our investment and travel capabilities. Our Kingsdale marketplace also directly challenged companies like Sears and American Express, which offered a portfolio of financial services.

Fisher thought that by offering additional services, the bank would be like a financial-services department store: You would attract more customers and they would buy more things. It was certainly a worthwhile concept, but in practice it fizzled.

CHAPTER FIVE

'Uncommon Partnership'

Well into the 1960s and beyond, most U.S. banks were limited by state laws to doing business in a single county. (Things were even more restrictive in Illinois, where banks were limited to a single branch, period. Not bad if you're in a metropolitan area with lots of customers like Chicago, but a real handicap if you're in Cairo or Cicero.) The federal Glass-Steagall Act, which separated investment banking and commercial banking activities, also limited M&A activity in the financial services sector. It was repealed in 1999.

Ohio had the single-county rule, though the law had been relaxed during the Depression years to allow for failing banks to be acquired by stronger ones here and there. In Ohio and elsewhere, then, small banks in rural counties had very limited growth potential. There was little competition among local banks, and none at all among banks in different counties. The result was too many small, potentially vulnerable banks and too much inefficiency in the banking system.

In the late 1960s, John G. devised a plan to sidestep these regulations prohibiting most in-state mergers. As the president of the smallest of three banks in an urban county, he rightly envisioned greener pastures in the small towns (and eventually larger cities) of Ohio. To him, artificial boundaries stopping banks at the county line just didn't make sense.

Father had already done some acquisitions within Franklin County, buying banks in the Columbus suburbs of Gahanna, Hilliard, Reynoldsburg and Westerville. What he learned from this was that while he could have built his own branches in these communities, it was so much better and more efficient to buy an established bank. You not only had built-in deposits, loans and customers, but you took away a competitor at the same time.

Together with Ev Reese, he came up with the idea of having a bank holding company—a corporate body that was not technically a bank and thus could lawfully expand across county and eventually state lines. Holding companies were not new, they were just not widely used for the purpose of bank mergers up to that point. City National's holding company, formed in October 1967, was called First Banc Group of Ohio, and its "holding" was City National Bank & Trust. The unusual spelling "Banc" was in keeping with an Ohio law that prohibited holding companies from calling themselves "banks." A fine point, to be sure.

Other states had the same requirement. Even today we see lots of holding companies with the "banc" spelling, while the customer-facing name of their branches remains "bank." A perfect example in Columbus is the holding company Huntington Bancshares Inc., doing business as Hunting-

◄ *Previous page:* Father and his right-hand-man, Everett Reese *(right)*, participating in a ribbon cutting ceremony for the new company headquarters at 100 E. Broad St. in Columbus. Ev was skilled at convincing small-town bankers throughout Ohio to sell their banks. Local managers and board members stayed on, an arrangement known as the "Uncommon Partnership."

Here's the Deal

ton National Bank. (The holding company structure allows Huntington and others to operate all sorts of non-banking businesses—selling insurance and mutual funds, for example—separately from their highly regulated banking operations.)

With the holding company structure in place, the stage was set for a new phase of growth. Father and Reese worked as a team, with Reese using his vast network of connections to put out feelers and make introductions for father. Reese knew everybody in all the banks in Ohio, which is one reason John G. wanted him at City National. Reese would send letters and make periodic phone calls to bank presidents, offering to meet should they ever be interested in selling. He also put the word out at banking conventions. You just never knew when the time would be right for a potential seller.

In 1968, Reese arranged for John G. to meet with the directors of Farmers Savings & Trust ($55.2 million in deposits), a county-seat bank in Mansfield, Ohio, located three counties to the north of Columbus. The directors of Farmers Savings were nearing retirement and looking to sell the company. Father and Ev drove to Mansfield to meet them.

"This fella named Nail—he ran an insurance business—said, 'Why don't you just tell us what you're going to pay?'" father told a writer for *Institutional Investor*. "I said, 'Mr. Nail, we're not going to buy your bank. If you want to merge, fine, but that's why we're here—to find out what assets you've got and we've got so we can come to an agreement.' He said, 'I don't believe it.' So I said, 'Okay, boys, let's go home—there's no reason to stand here.' And one of their guys said, 'C'mon now, Mr. McCoy, why don't you just stay here a minute and we'll talk.'"

He stayed, they talked, and Farmers Savings agreed to the deal, with the bank's management staying in place along with its board of directors. It was City National's first acquisition outside of Franklin County.

First Banc Group's second transaction was the 1971 acquisition of Security Central National Bank of Portsmouth, Ohio, way down at the southern tip of the state along the Ohio River. Once again, Reese made the introduction and father gave the presentation, running through the innovative prod-ucts City National had developed and the important role local people would play after the sale. As part of his pitch he could now point to the Mansfield transaction as a model for how things would be done.

In similar fashion, Ev and father continued to acquire small banks around Ohio. Between 1968 and 1980 the holding company bought twenty-two banks, each under $100m in assets. These were financial institutions with deep roots in their communities and a focus on small business and individ-uals. Because City National was retail to the core, going after small-town banks—regardless of what county they were in—made a lot more sense to us than it did to our commercial-bank competitors. That's how we got such a big head start on bigger banks in the M&A game. Our competitors probably thought father was nuts to be spending money on seemingly inconsequential banks, and it turned out he was crazy—like a fox.

What was in it for the sellers? These were old-school bankers who didn't know anything about data-processing, credit cards or automobile leasing, forces that were changing the banking industry. In one fell swoop, the sellers got needed technical expertise, management support and back-up lending ability.

Unlike most other acquirers, City National wanted local management to stay on, and they usually did. If a few people wanted to retire, then so be it. The banks retained their local names, boards of directors and a great degree of management autonomy. Keeping the local infrastructure became a hall-mark of First Banc Group and later Banc One Corp. We had a special name for it—the "Uncommon Partnership"—another memorable phrase turned by Fisher in 1968.

The Uncommon Partnership was a decentralized system for running our banks. Sellers retained a high degree of local identity and control of custom-er-facing operations. What father did centralize was data processing, account-ing and other unseen "back office" functions, which most sellers were happy to give up. We let the local people make installment loans and offer our credit

Here's the Deal

cards to their customers. If it involved people, we did it locally; if it involved paper, we did it centrally.

First with City National under father and later with me leading Banc One, the Uncommon Partnership was very much a competitive advantage in negotiating deals. It celebrated the local people instead of casting them aside. Our goal was to help them become better bankers.

Here is how father described City National's unique approach in a news release announcing one of his acquisitions: "We have been successful because we free local bankers from paperwork to enable them to be more effective with people work. Basically, our philosophy enables each of our banks to concentrate on better identifying the unique needs of the community it serves and to meet those needs with the sophisticated tools we provide."

To which the president of the newly acquired bank added: "Banking is in the early stages of a revolution. ... We wanted to maintain the freedom to respond to our customers while obtaining additional resources and technological expertise." Being acquired by First Banc Group "was the best answer," the bank president concluded.

The Uncommon Partnership was not a gimmick or a publicity stunt, it was good business. We felt that banks are people businesses, and the local bankers knew all the people. Even if we had wanted to throw out the locals, we were growing so fast in the 1970s and '80s that we didn't have enough manpower in Columbus to send out and run all these banks. And a great side benefit of M&A was that quite often we learned things from the banks we acquired, which was healthy for the entire organization.

Most of our competitors had a very different approach. Ohio National Bank and Huntington, for example, would basically go in and say, "We're going to buy your bank and tell you how to run it. Or better yet, we'll run it for you." They might have put a gentler spin on things, but that was how it worked. In those cases, the sellers were looking for the highest price and were not particularly concerned about the future, because they weren't going to be around to experience it. The buyers were looking to acquire market share and generate efficiencies by cutting costs and headcount.

We were much more people friendly, and it appealed to certain sellers. The president knew we weren't going to fire him, and there was a real possibility that we would be adding local people. So it came down to this: Would you rather sell to us and keep your people and board of directors, or sell to one of the other guys and be gone? The choice was that simple. And with every successful acquisition we made, our sales pitch to prospective sellers got easier. Our record spoke for itself.

In 1983 I became president of the holding company and went from having twenty branches in Franklin County reporting to me, to twenty-six banks in Ohio under my jurisdiction. By this time, we were starting to see some of the limitations of a decentralized management system. The Uncommon Partnership needed a few tweaks as the bank continued to grow.

Remember that each of these approximately two dozen affiliates had its own local president, most often the same person who had run the bank for a decade or more before the acquisition. Now they were reporting to the thirty-nine-year-old son of the CEO with a Stanford MBA. You really can't blame them for being skeptical. I would have doubted me, too!

As we had grown, the holding company was in need of more consistency in budgeting and growth forecasting. What I needed to do was to get my hands around these individual banks and develop a system of best practices that would spell out common procedures that everyone would follow, in every market. Not to undo the local control of the Uncommon Partnership system, but to institute systems that we all could follow when it came to making loans or reaching sales projections within our budget. What could I do, for example, to avoid having affiliates in twenty-six different markets making loan projections twenty-six different ways? That was my challenge.

What I came up with was a management information system that we called "Share and Compare." You might call it the "Uncommon Partnership

2.0," because it shared the same basic philosophy of local control but with a lot more detail and accountability.

The inspiration came from John Reed, a Citicorp official who in 1984 became CEO of that company. In the early 1970s Reed was an upper-level Citicorp official, serving on the board of a Columbus-area computer time-sharing company called Management Horizons Data Systems, founded by an Ohio State University professor named William Arthur "Art" Cullman. (Cullman's brother Joseph was a former CEO of the Philip Morris tobacco company.) MHDS automated various functions of companies, things like accounting or human resources, to help executives manage a business more efficiently.

Reed was a techie, a numbers guy and a management guru. Raised in Argentina and Brazil by his American parents, Reed joined Citicorp when data processing was in its infancy, and he helped the bank build its technological capabilities. Like my father and Fisher, he was an early champion of the ATM.

We would occasionally cross paths at banking conferences, and at one point he mentioned what he was doing with Management Horizons. We sometimes got together when he was in Columbus, and we have remained friendly all these years.

Reed was greatly influenced by what all these Ohio State University professors were cooking up at Management Horizons. He believed that Citicorp could sell more loans if the bank could forecast tendencies about the companies they were calling on. MHDS was a consulting business that did a lot of numbers crunching and provided Reed with some of this information. Using MHDS data, he could look at how much product a company sold on a Monday or a Thursday, and forecast with relative certainty how much they would sell on a Monday or a Thursday six months in the future. Today we call this predictive analytics.

So what did all this mean to me? Reed convinced me that by using these predictive techniques, we could become more analytical at how we looked at our branches and affiliate banks, ultimately improving the accuracy of our forecasting at the holding company level. This is the secret sauce that really differentiated us from the competition. I can't overemphasize that point.

For example, if I went to one of my bank presidents and said, "How much growth are you expecting next year?" he would most likely pull a figure out of his hat—like every other banker in the industry at that time—that was based on past history and his feel for the local economy. "Six percent growth," he might say. If I countered that maybe we could do better, he'd say, "OK, seven percent."

Any way you looked at it, this was a guessing game, based more on intuition than facts and figures. Share and Compare changed all that. This is what made us so successful.

Let's say we had an annual goal of ten percent loan growth across the holding company. We needed a measurable plan that spelled out how all the banks would get there.

To increase a $100 million loan portfolio by ten percent, you need to loan $110 million. Let's say the average loan is $1 million, so you've got 100 loans on the books. And if the average loan pays off in six months, you also need to account for that turnover. You have to make new loans and replace the loans that are paid off.

In this fashion we started budgeting. What is your average loan size, how many loans will be paid off, how many new loans do you need to make, etc.

I could go into an affiliate bank on the fifteenth of the month and say, "How are you doing?" And if the president said, "Well, it's going great, it feels pretty good," I could respond, "No, how many loans have you made? To make your budget this month you have to make 30 loans. How many have you made?"

If he said, "I've made two in fifteen days," he probably wasn't going to make twenty-eight more in the next fifteen days.

Another component of Share and Compare was peer review. We divided the banks by size—under $100 million in assets, $100 million to $1 billion, and over $1 billion. Every month we would compile all the numbers for each bank and compare everybody to everybody else. Then I could go into a particular bank and say, "Gee, you only did ten loans this month." The local president might say that's all they could do. And I could say that three similar banks within thirty miles each did twenty-five loans, or whatever the case might be. That put an end to any quibbling because nobody wanted to be last in their peer group. And because there were a number of others that were doing better, it was hard to argue that he couldn't improve.

Likewise, if we acquired a new bank and it had more employees than necessary, I wouldn't go to them as say, "I think you ought to fire twenty percent of your people." If I did that, it would only make them mad, and for all I knew they might go and fire their best people, just to spite me. It was far more effective to let the numbers do the talking. After several months had passed, I might go the CFO or president and say, "In commercial lending, you have one person for every $1 million in assets. The average for all our banks is one person per $1.8 million, and the best one is $2.1 million."

I might also suggest that he go and visit with these three top-performing banks and see how they're doing things. Before long the new guy would conclude that he had to get rid of twenty percent of his people, and he could rightly take all the credit when profitability improved. (When he had gotten it done he could come back to me and boast about being in the top tier of our banks. He'd be proud because he had done it on his own.)

Because the local banks had so much freedom, a lot of the new and good ideas came from the local banks and not from headquarters. We would always try to find a couple things a newly acquired bank was doing differently that we could put into our other banks. We didn't think we had a monopoly on all the good ideas in the world, and this really helped to build teams.

I'm sure the laggards struggled with Share and Compare, but we tried to be teachers as opposed to dictators. We gave them ways to figure it out. The system provided a framework while leaving execution to the local affiliates. It was designed to help people improve themselves. Most important of all, share and compare was effective because it created a healthy competition among affiliate banks. They all wanted to win.

As the bank grew, senior management needed more efficient ways to keep our fingers on the pulse of the business. Another innovation of Share and Compare was requiring each bank president to send me a one-page memo three days after the end of each month, telling me how they were doing on a macro level. I wanted to know what was good, what was bad, were they going to make their numbers for the quarter, that sort of detail. But it had to be one page or less! It forced them to be concise and hit the high points, but it let me know what issues we faced in the coming months.

One local president, in his first report to headquarters, took my brevity requirement and ran with it. "Everything's fine," he wrote. Period. End of report.

I slammed the paper down on my desk and sort of went berserk. "Who does he think he is?" I said to my CFO at the time.

"Relax John," the CFO said. "If everything's fine, why should you care?" I begrudgingly conceded the point.

The Share and Compare system absolutely changed the dynamics of how we looked at the business, making our operations very analytical. And while it might not sound revolutionary today, it was groundbreaking then. It really drove our success and profitability during my time as CEO, starting in 1984.

CHAPTER SIX

Bank What?

$\mathcal{N}$ow we've arrived at the question I'm asked probably more than any other: How did we come up with the name *Bank One*? It's a pretty entertaining story.

Before I answer, let me explain why City National, the bank, and First Banc Group of Ohio, the holding company, needed a rebranding.

When father bought those very first banks in the Franklin County suburbs, their names were changed to City National. That seemed to make the most business sense in a market where we were already known. But when father ventured into other counties, he did not convert local bank names to City National. In those instances, John G. felt that the continuity of the local name, and retention of local management, had greater value in distant markets.

Over time and as the pace of acquisitions increased, having multiple bank names operating under one holding company roof became unwieldy. By 1977, First Banc Group had sixteen members and $1.95 billion in aggregate assets.

Customer service was the main factor. Once we acquired a bank, we could service that customer in any City National branch or any of the other banks owned by our holding company. Early in the acquisitions process, when member banks were several counties apart, this wasn't an issue. But when we had a bunch of banks with different names—sometimes a few miles apart—our own customers didn't know they could get service in one of these affiliate banks with a different name. That didn't make much sense for us or them.

So with customer convenience and future expansion in mind, senior management decided to unify marketing efforts by having all of its member banks adopt similar names. But what name?

One day in early 1979, father instructed Fisher to come up with a new name for the bank, something catchy and well-suited for new markets, whether rural or urban. One that could quite conceivably be crossing state lines at some point in the near future, when being associated with a physical location could be a liability (How many folks in Ann Arbor, Michigan would open an account at First Buckeye Bank and Trust?).

Fisher's reply? "I've got the name."

John G. was taken aback. "Well, what is it?" he inquired.

"Bank One."

"Bank *what?*"

"Bank One," Fisher repeated.

It was certainly catchy, at a minimum brash and bordering on arrogant. Especially in an industry where tradition, stability and sense of place were the

◄ *Previous page:* Changing the bank's name from City National to Bank One took some getting used to for most people. Full-page newspaper ads like this one ran in both Columbus newspapers at the time.

norm. *National Bank of Detroit, Manufacturers Hanover Trust, Bank of America, First Federal Savings and Loan.* Not a gimmicky group.

Could we really be Bank One? The one and only, the bank before all others, the number one bank in…the entire universe?

Father mulled the name, letting it roll around his tongue like a baby getting a first taste of solid food. Hmm, not bad, he thought. In fact, he rather liked it. Here was a man, after all, who had hired Phyllis Diller to star in his commercials.

Now to sell it to the board.

"If it's you alone who came up with it, a lot of people will shoot it down," father advised Fisher. "Go out and get an opinion."

Fisher hired a New York advertising agency to come up with and test a bunch of potential names. Over several weeks, the agency did a series of interviews with senior managers, starting with 50 or so names and carefully whittling down the list.

"What's your favorite of this group? How does this one make you feel? What don't you like about that one?" It was a process of elimination, without letting on about which ones were being eliminated. Father and Fisher made sure that Bank One was always among the active names.

Was it a fair process? I'm really not sure. One thing I do know is that when it comes to marketing, everyone thinks they are an expert. Nobody in senior management or on a board of directors can create a computer program for you, but ask ten of them about marketing or branding or slogans, and you'll get ten different "expert" opinions.

What father and Fisher wanted to avoid was having it come down to three finalists with everybody disagreeing. Their plan was to present a single name that they could say had been tested, vetted and approved, and that was going to be our new name. Case closed.

Roughly two months after the process began, they were ready to reveal the name to the board. Not offer or suggest, but reveal. John G. asked Fisher to do the honors.

"Gentlemen, based on all the studies we've done and subject to rigorous testing, we have come up with a new name for our company: Bank One."

A brief silence was broken by a cascade of grunts and groans.

"Bank ONE? Oh REALLY? It's awful! Eeww!" were among the catcalls.

After the initial outburst, all eyes fell on John Galbreath, a legendary real estate developer, owner of the Pittsburgh Pirates and the most respected man on the board, if not in all of Columbus and possibly Ohio. Surely, sensible Mr. Galbreath, who was eighty-two at the time, would put a stop to this Bank One madness.

He leaned forward. "It's magnificent!" he crowed. The room was quiet.

Father seized the moment, smacked the palm of his hand on the conference table and declared, "Then that's going to be our name!"

Bank One it was.

Thereafter, the holding company would be known as Banc One Corp., and each bank as Bank One followed by its location. Thus City National Bank became Bank One Columbus, Farmers Saving & Trust became Bank One Mansfield and Security Central National Bank became Bank One Portsmouth.

With a new name, a good story to tell prospective sellers and demonstrated success in integrating acquisitions, the bank was entering a new phase. Between 1980 and 1983, Banc One began to purchase midsize banks in larger markets. In rapid succession, Banc One bought banks in the Cleveland (Lake County National Bank; Bank One Painesville), Akron (Firestone Bank; Bank One Akron) and Youngstown (Union National Bank; Bank One Youngstown) markets. For those unfamiliar with Ohio geography, these banks were generally in the northeastern part of the state, a largely urban, industrial and populous region stretching from Lake Erie to the Pennsylvania and West Virginia state lines. It was also the backyard of two of our largest Ohio competitors, National City and Ameritrust Bank, both headquartered in Cleveland.

In June 1982, father and Havens made a bold move that got the attention of not just our in-state competitors but the entire banking industry, by announcing the acquisition of Dayton-based Winters National Bank & Trust. It would be our largest acquisition to date, extending Banc One's reach all the way to Cincinnati in southwestern Ohio while strengthening us in existing markets.

Established by the grandfather of comedian Jonathan Winters, Winters National Bank had $1.6 billion in assets (to our $5.4 billion), operating forty-two branches in the greater Dayton area, one in Cincinnati, three in Circleville (south of Columbus) and twenty-one Euclid National Bank branch offices in the Cleveland area. The $122 million transaction was the largest to date in Ohio, creating the number one financial institution in the state with assets of $7 billion (though we still trailed Ohio National, recently rebraned as BancOhio, and were about even with Huntington in our home market of Columbus). More importantly, the Winters deal created the first real statewide bank in Ohio, validated our Uncommon Partnership philosophy and positioned Banc One for its next phase of growth outside of Ohio when I would become CEO a year later.

(An aside: At dinner one night before a board meeting in these early years, I found myself seated with three of our older directors: Leonard Firestone, the son of tire magnate Harvey Firestone, who joined our board when we bought Firestone Bank in Akron; Virginia Kettering, the daughter of Charles "Boss" Kettering, inventor of the electric automobile starter as research chief for General Motors, who came to us when we bought Winters Bank in Dayton; and John Galbreath. Somehow we got into a debate over who was friendlier—Wilbur or Orville Wright. All three of them actually were acquainted with the legendary aviation pioneers from Dayton. After a few minutes of back and forth, everyone agreed that Wilbur was indeed friendlier than Orville. You read it here first.)

How did the Winters deal happen? Winters was a large bank and a market leader, but very much an average performer. We were just the opposite—a high performer whose stock was trading at a premium to our peers. Both companies were publicly traded entities but Winters' stock traded at a much lower multiple than ours because we were more profitable (the multiple is represented by the price-to-earnings, or P/E, ratio of a stock—the price divided by the earnings per share. The higher the P/E ratio, the more valuable the stock as a currency). So if they were going to be competing with Banc One for acquisitions, we would have the advantage because our currency—our stock—was worth more than theirs, and we could afford to pay more for acquisitions than they could. That was the case then and continues to be true today. The companies with the most highly valued stock—not necessarily the highest-priced stock—generally have the upper hand.

Winters management was getting older and they knew very well that they couldn't compete for deals with the largest and best-run banks. So who would they rather sell to, a bank that was going to kick management to the curb and dissolve their board, or one that was going to keep their people and let them continue to be the most important bankers in their market? And make them a lot of money as Banc One continued to grow and its stock gained value. They chose to negotiate a deal with us.

After the Winters acquisition, Banc One never looked back. Less than a year later, father retired and I became CEO in addition to president. Federal and state barriers to bank acquisitions across state lines were about to fall, and Banc One was ready for its next and most explosive phase of growth.

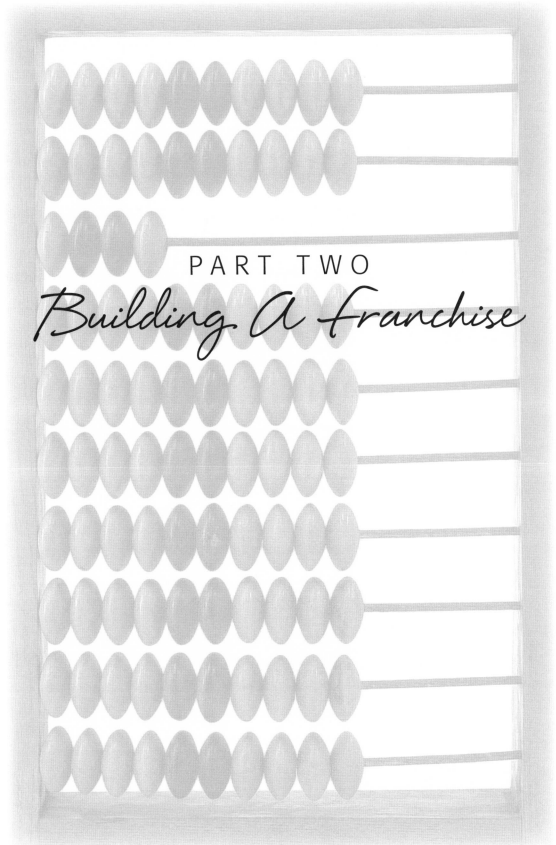

PART TWO

Building A Franchise

CHAPTER SEVEN

My Life and Times

We didn't feel rich growing up, but of course we were privileged. Dad was by no means a spendthrift and he had the distinction of being a banker who didn't want his children to go into debt.

One summer, my sister Jinny earned $400 teaching and told father she wanted to spend $300 of it for a tape player and new speakers for her car. "Why would you want to do that?" he inquired. "What else could you do with that money?" When she was in college she bought a black and white TV from Sears through an installment loan, making payments over several months with interest figured in. "Father was mortified," she recalled.

Dad was careful not to forbid us from doing something, preferring to let us draw certain conclusions ourselves. Early in my career at the bank, when I was running the commercial lending department, I attended a seminar in

New York sponsored by Citicorp. There were various suggestions about how to build a profitable loan portfolio, and Sweden was one of the countries singled out for opportunities. The conference leader said Sweden was a peaceful country with a stable currency in the Krona and high interest rates, three desirable traits for lenders.

When I returned to Columbus, I enthusiastically suggested to father that we make international loans. "Great," he said. "What countries do you like?"

"Sweden," I replied.

"Fantastic!" he said, reaching for his coat and hat. "I'm going to lunch now, so why don't you take the next hour and write down everything you know about Sweden and why you like it so much. I'll take a look when I get back."

He left, and after about thirty seconds I realized I didn't know anything about Sweden. That was the end of that.

Sure, it stung, but I learned two lessons. The first was that in banking, you don't rush into anything you don't understand. That applies to products as well as markets. Secondly, my relationship with John G. was this double-edged sword that both helped and hurt me throughout my career. He was going to hold me to a higher standard to blunt charges of nepotism, and yet I had this incredible insight into his thinking and access to him during work and after hours. It was my decision to return to City National to work for father, so it was up to me to deal with the negatives and take full advantage of my opportunities.

There were maybe five or six really rich families in Columbus when I was growing up. Two of them were the Wolfes, who owned Ohio National Bank, The Ohio Company regional stock brokerage, *The Columbus Dispatch* newspaper and vast acres of farmland acquired for pennies on the dollar during the Depression; and the Galbreaths, another family dynasty led by real estate developer John Galbreath, who built office buildings around the country, owned the Pittsburgh Pirates and bred world-class racehorses on a

◀ *Previous page:* The former Jane Deborah Taylor emerges from Stanford Memorial Church in Palo Alto, California for the first time as Mrs. John B. McCoy on April 21, 1968.

splendid farm on the western outskirts of Franklin County, where Columbus is located. As I mentioned, father was fortunate to have John Galbreath on the board of City National.

Compared to these families, we felt pretty ordinary, but we had many advantages. Educational opportunities and a network of friends in high places were among them.

Bexley schools were excellent then as now, but mother and father sent me to Columbus Academy, a private college preparatory school. There were twenty-two people in my graduating class, all boys. I was class president my senior year and have remained close with a number of my former classmates and their families. My sister Jinny spent a number of years at the private Columbus School for Girls but attended the public Bexley High School for four years.

Because Columbus Academy and Bexley are both on the East Side of Columbus, the schools had quite a friendly rivalry in academics, sports and social affairs. Sort of a rich kids' rivalry, you could say. They called us the Tweeds because we wore coats and ties, and we called them the Toads, because it annoyed them. It was a very tame version of West Side Story's Jets and Sharks gangs, without the leather, switchblades or song and dance numbers.

The Academy really prepared me for college, with loads of reading and writing. I most definitely gained a curiosity about the world, which is what a good education should provide.

I visited a fair number of colleges and universities, and never really considered the 800-pound gorilla right in my back yard, The Ohio State University. I was used to a much smaller institution and was hankering to see another part of the country—and quite honestly, put some distance between myself and my parents. I'm sure I wasn't the first nineteen-year-old to feel that way!

Why Williams College? For starters, I knew I wanted to go east. I visited Yale and Princeton, and while they are fantastic institutions, I found them to be too big and stuffy. (I got locked out of my room following a late night out at Yale and received a stern lecture in the wee hours from a grumpy janitor. I wonder if that ever happened to either of the Presidents Bush?)

Williams felt different. It was the first school that I visited and I had a wonderful time, attending one of the great fraternity parties of my young life. I compared all the other schools to Williams, and they didn't measure up for me.

While I supposedly was an above-average student, there was little evidence of it during my first two years at Williams. It's not that I was dumb or incapable. Looking back, I just wasn't that interested—uninspired might be the best way to say it. I definitely was more active socially than academically. (I eventually served on the board of Williams College and received an honorary Doctor of Laws degree in 1992. Not bad for a kid who had been on "social probation" while he was in school!)

After my sophomore year I was basically a C-plus student. My father was very good because he didn't take a long time to say anything. "What are you going to do when you graduate?" he asked one day, and I said I'd probably go to Harvard or Stanford. "With *those* grades?"

That's all he had to say. I got the message and hit the books. I finished on the honor roll and was fortunate enough to be accepted at Stanford.

It was in graduate school that I finally hit my stride. I began to figure out that I really wanted to go into business. Not necessarily banking, but definitely business.

Stanford certainly challenged me intellectually. It was there that I learned to have an open mind and work collaboratively with others. The big difference between Williams and Stanford was the team approach.

At Williams, you'd write a paper and it was all independent work and thought. You could go on for fifty pages and nobody would challenge you. Look mom, I can write!

Stanford was the exact opposite. They'd take five of us and say, "Get together and write a two-page paper on this topic," which might sound easy but is pretty hard to do. There was no particular right approach to the problem, but everyone in the group had to agree. Instead of trying to beat the other guy, you were trying to work with the other guy and get a better result. That is the essence of collaboration. It was a valuable lesson that guided me throughout my career.

Undergraduate work was like being a soloist while graduate school was being a member of the marching band. The latter required movement in a common direction. Above all, graduate school was what business was like.

My social life was flourishing at Stanford. I met my future wife on a blind date. Jane Taylor, a beautiful graduate student in education. When people say opposites attract, they might have us in mind. Jane and I are best friends and a perfect complement to one another, even if we sometimes disagree and gravitate toward different social causes and political parties. On more than one occasion Janie has been known to wag a finger at me and proclaim, "Don't you John G. me!" when I'm being bossy and not considering her perspective on something. That always makes us both laugh. I'm pleased to report that at this writing we have three wonderful children and eight happy and healthy grandchildren, so life is good. And in April 2018, we celebrated our fiftieth wedding anniversary. Janie has been, without a doubt, the smartest "investment" I've ever made.

While Jane's idea of a perfect Saturday afternoon is a walk in the woods or a stroll on a beach, mine is more likely to involve a round of golf or watching the Ohio State Buckeyes. (And yes, I do have season tickets.) Since I've mentioned Ohio State football, let me digress. Although I didn't attend "The" Ohio State University, you can't grow up and spend most of your working adult life in Columbus, Ohio and not be at least a casual OSU football fan. Let me be clear: I am more than a casual fan.

People like to call Columbus the largest college town in America, and they would be correct. OSU is one of the largest universities in the country with 65,000 students and sits less than three miles from downtown. With no major league football, basketball or baseball (Columbus has had pro hockey and soccer for some time now) to divert attention from college sports, the Buckeyes—and we're talking primarily football—have been the hottest sports tickets in town for 125 years and counting.

When I was running the company, Banc One always had a box and dozens of season tickets at Ohio Stadium. We'd sponsor a lunch for 100-125 customers before every home game and charter buses to take everyone to the stadium. The box only held 18 people, and that was reserved for our best customers, husbands and wives. Because I played host, Janie had to go to every home football game, generally eight per season. That's a lot of football for a California outdoorsy type who'd rather be wearing a backpack than watching a quarterback.

Janie is nothing if not a gamer, however, and polite in the extreme. She faithfully upheld her duties as wife of the CEO, but always positioned herself at the far end of the second row of the box, where she could safely peruse a copy of *Time* magazine stashed within the official game program on her lap. She was very well trained in this exercise and would jump up and cheer when everyone else did, even if she didn't have a clue about what had just transpired on the field.

All the guests were impressed by her apparent obsession with statistics and other program trivia, never suspecting the subterfuge. It's interesting how things change, because during the Buckeyes' 2014-15 season title run, it was Janie who insisted that we attend the national championship game in Dallas. Over time, she really became a fan of the game.

When I graduated from Stanford in 1967, the Vietnam War was in full swing. The reality was, once graduate school was over, I was probably going to have to join the service unless I got a deferment by working toward another degree. Once again, father made his feelings known with the fewest words possible: "Do you think you can *afford* to get a Ph.D.?"

So the military it would be. Like many young people in those days, I had my trepidations about Vietnam. It didn't seem like the smartest or most necessary engagement for our country. But I was no conscientious objector or flag-burning protestor. I felt like you owed it to your country to serve, but like anything else, if I had to serve I wanted to find something I wanted to do.

A little research turned up a hospital administration program in the U.S. Air Force. Because I had a master's degree in business, I could qualify for a direct commission in the Air Force as a first lieutenant. I enlisted and was sent to Sheppard Air Force Base in Wichita Falls, Texas, for training as a hospital administrator.

One day in the course of training, our class of approximately 30 officers was given a so-called dream sheet of military bases where we'd like to be stationed. Everyone got up to three choices, then it was up to the Air Force to decide.

My first choice was Washington, D.C., because I like big cities and also thought it would be a good career move and learning experience to be around as much brass as possible. It has never bothered me to be around important people because that's when you have the best chance of getting big decisions made quickly. It's also a great way to learn how things are done, why certain actions are being taken or postponed, and what's really going on. There is no better window on the world of power than being around the decision makers.

Another digression: I used to attend the Association of Reserve City Bankers, an annual conference for the top 100 U.S. banks. The events were a combination of policymaking, politicking and socializing. Over a three or four day period, the bankers would have meetings in the mornings and generally a round of golf in the afternoons. I started to notice that no one was inviting the CEOs from the largest three or four banks to play golf. I guess the smaller bank CEOs were too intimidated by the big guys, or didn't think the CEOs of Bank of America or JPMorgan would want to join their parties. And because the top executives were so competitive with each other, none of them would take the initiative to invite each other, so they were missing out on all the action.

It got to be so absurd that John Reed of Citicorp would call me up. "John, when's our golf game this year?" The point was, he didn't have one, and was relying on me to make it happen for him. At this time Banc One was a top fifteen or twenty bank, but I took it upon myself to call the CEOs of the largest banks and coordinate a round of golf between them (myself included, of course). They loved to play with the other top guys, because that's where they could share their experiences and get lots of information. And I benefited because I got to hear what all the top CEOs were talking about. Those exclusive rounds became a tradition, and I always had my seat at the table as the event organizer.

While we are on the subject, let me explain what you might call my obsession with golf. I've always enjoyed sports, be it skiing, squash or paddle tennis. But golf really is a game you can do for almost your entire life. And you can learn quite a lot about someone while playing golf. If I was hiring a senior person and found that they played golf, I'd always try to organize a game. In eighteen holes you learn how competitive a person is, and how he or she handles stress and strife.

One guy I was attempting to hire hit into the rough and moved his ball twice on the first hole. I didn't need to play the next seventeen holes because I already knew this wasn't the type of person I would hire at my company. If he'd cheat for a two dollar bet, what would he do in a business situation?

While I didn't particularly enjoy business golf because it took so long, golf with my best buddies was a way I could relax after a difficult week. My good friends were not necessarily great business people and couldn't care less about what I was doing in business. We'd just get out there and yack it up for five hours and unwind. And even at my current age, golf is important to my body and mind, and I remain chairman of the PGA Tour board.

Back to the military. If I was going to be in the Air Force and run something, I might as well be in the thick of things. Put me in the company of chieftains any day. I always want to be with the decision makers.

I think a lot of my classmates were hoping for just the opposite, maybe so they could fly under the radar. This is a natural tendency in most people and it explains why the front rows of classrooms and conference halls usually sit empty as everybody fills in from the back with their Starbucks and smart phones in hand, safely out of the intellectual line of fire.

Because no one else chose Washington, I ended up being the only one to be awarded his first choice. Perfect.

In the fall of 1967, at the ripe age of twenty-four, I took up duties as a squadron commander at Andrews Air Force Base, in charge of 1,500 enlisted service members, male and female, working in various military hospitals and other health facilities in the D.C. area. Was I in over my head? Maybe just a little.

Sergeant Major William Jesse was thin as a rail and smoked like a chimney. A career military man with twenty-eight years of service under his belt, he was now reporting to me, with all of three months' experience in the Air Force. He knew his job backwards and forwards; I still needed directions to the men's room. This was not a person I was going to boss around and live to tell about it.

I'll never forget our first meeting. "If you stay out of my way, you're really going to enjoy this," he informed me. And, boy, was he right.

I did stay out of Sgt. Jesse's way, and once we got to know each other, we were a great team. Often we'd play golf in the morning and end up at the racetrack at night. He kept me out of trouble and several times I protected him.

The only thing he couldn't save me from was the monthly base parade I was required to march in, leading about sixty other squad members with voice commands and gestures. Despite being a pretty good dancer, I struggled mightily to keep time in those parades. If I were the Ohio State Marching Band drum major leading the famous *Script Ohio* routine, in which the band spells out "Ohio," I'm sure we'd end up spelling "Oreo" or "Ontario."

The military was three great years of learning, my first full-time job and first real management experience. I realized that there were some capable folks and not-so-capable folks who were reporting to me, and it was my responsibility to help them to be the best soldiers, hospital professionals and people that they could be. No manager gets all A players, so maximizing the potential of those around you is essential to your success and that of others. That's true in the military, banking or anyplace else. You find the right people and let them lead. I had my man in Sgt. Jesse and couldn't have succeeded without him.

Working effectively with senior figures became my calling card. The collaborative approach to leadership was clearly my comfort zone, and with very few exceptions it worked extremely well for me throughout my banking career.

Fresh out of the Air Force, I was given increasingly complex roles at City National and First Banc Group with less experience than most of my reports, and later became CEO of Banc One Corp. at forty-one. It's nearly impossible for any executive, politician or military person to walk into a room and command instant authority when you're perceived as a greenhorn. Remember that father had brought in a seasoned executive in Ev Reese when he was young and starting out, to lend him the gravitas he lacked in dealing with his peers. While John G. later embraced the top-down management style in keeping with his era, I rarely resorted to the "my way or the highway" tactics of traditional CEOs, aiming to be more of a teacher than a dictator.

While I was still in the military, Jane and I married on April 21, 1968. With the country in turmoil—anti-war demonstrations, political assassinations and race riots were all too common—our new life together was relative calm in a rough sea.

We lived in the Washington suburb of Oxon Hill, Maryland. It was not an upscale part of town. We had virtually no money and lived on the top floor of a three-story building cooled by the Pee-wee Herman of air conditioners. If it was 106 degrees outside, our apartment would be 100.

When I was preparing to leave the service, my father asked me what I wanted to do. I said I'd like to work at a bank like Citicorp, where I could establish myself and get some credentials. I had spent two summers working in New York during graduate school, and there was no more exciting place for a young professional with no children.

"Would you ever come back to Columbus?" he inquired one day. Having just been accepted for a training program with Citicorp in New York, I hesitated.

At that time, Citicorp was far and away the foremost bank in the United States, and their bankers were the best, brightest and smartest in the business. If you worked for Citicorp in those days, you moved every two years, and I mean all over the world. Once I asked a Citicorp veteran what it was like working there, and he said, "Well, John, it was tough. When you go to your first meeting you stand in the corner so they could only come at you from three different ways." As the song says, if you could make it there, the thought was you could make it anywhere.

Yet I was also interested in working for my father. I loved Columbus and I loved my friends in Columbus. The issue was how to prove myself. I thought Citicorp would provide that crucial space and training.

I told father that if I spent some time with Citicorp, I'd learn all kinds of things—commercial lending and international banking—that could be put to good use at City National.

He thought about that for an instant. "What if you're the best person in the world making shipping loans to the Greeks," he began. "We're never going to be making shipping loans to the Greeks. Better to come to Columbus and learn this business from the ground up."

Vintage father.

Jane and I discussed our options. She was (and remains) a California girl at heart. Innovative Bank of America notwithstanding, she understood that the California banks weren't of the quality of the eastern banks at that time. And we both agreed that New York loses some of its glamour for married folks planning to raise a family. There was no great intellectual discussion about Columbus. She readily agreed to move there.

After a short vacation to Greece and the former Yugoslavia with another couple (using money that Jane had earned substitute teaching), the military moved us to Columbus on September 30, 1970. Jane flew ahead while I tied up some loose ends in Washington. She stayed with my parents and looked for houses.

After one day of looking, she called and said she had found the perfect house. "You're going to love it. It has a swimming pool," she informed me.

I told her we couldn't afford a house with a swimming pool, but she insisted it was in our price range. It wasn't. There was no use in arguing and we bought the house, which also came with three bedrooms and a two-car garage. My professional journey had begun.

CHAPTER EIGHT

Working for Father

There were a number of good reasons to work for my father at City National Bank rather than take a job with Citicorp in New York, but salary wasn't one of them. I was pretty much a fish out of water at City National with my Stanford MBA, and could have made a lot more money at Citicorp. Father knew this and had a plan.

He told the board that he wanted to create a program that would enable him to hire MBAs, something only the largest banks in the country did on a consistent basis. He got board support to create a bank officers' training program, an innovative way for a small bank in Columbus to enrich its talent pool. Participants stayed in the program for three-to-five years, getting a new assignment every six-to-nine months and rotating between departments. Department heads loved it because father paid the salaries of the trainees from his office's budget, so we were basically free labor for any department we were assigned to. The inaugural class was a Harvard MBA and me. The Harvard guy was really smart but even then you could tell he was not cut out for management.

We were brought in as banking officers, which was an important distinction in those days, justifying a higher salary. Our starting salary was perhaps $12,000 a year, which would amount to about $40,000 today. (Freshly minted Stanford MBAs probably start at $75,000 to $100,000 these days.)

Even the "officer" title alone, absent the higher pay, was an inducement to young and ambitious MBAs. In hindsight, two new hires with MBAs sounds pretty unexceptional, but I'm certain that the big banks in Columbus—Ohio National and Huntington—didn't have Harvard and Stanford MBAs working for them. I was just grateful to get an opening into the business.

Father never wanted people to say that nepotism was behind my coming to the bank, so everything I did or became had to be on the merits. One thing we had to decide immediately was how I would address him. "Mr. McCoy" and "Hey Pops" were clearly out of the question. At work I always referred to him as "John G." and in private he was "Dad." He called me "John B." or "Johnny." Some of my detractors referred to father as "John the Good" or "John God," while I was "John the Bad" or "John Boy." The permutations were endless and at times a distraction. One thing my father and I agreed on: My son, John T., is "John Terrific."

Quite astutely and correctly, father decided that the best thing for him and for me was for us to be as far away from each other as possible. He worked downtown, so I was assigned to the bank's operations center eight miles away on the outskirts of town. It was a blessing.

My first day at City National is pretty much a blur, but I do remember going to the downtown office and being driven by the bank's president, Gor-

◄ *Previous page:* John G. McCoy, sometimes called "John God" or "John the Good" by admirers, was already a banking legend in Ohio and beyond when I came to work for him in 1970.

don Jelliffe, to the operations center north of town. Being delivered, like a fresh pizza, made me uncomfortable because I was certainly capable of getting there myself. Getting a lift—from the bank president, no less—sent the wrong signal to my co-workers, sort of like a spoiled rich kid being dropped off at day camp by the butler. I'm sure Jelliffe meant well and in any case it was a nice gesture on his part.

With thankfully little fanfare, Jelliffe handed me off to the company's chief financial officer, Bill Rutherford, who was very capable and great to work for. My first assignment, which lasted about nine months, was to learn the inner workings of the operations center. Lots of mundane but crucial things happened there, including all the permanent paperwork associated with opening and closing accounts. Every account had a ledger card, and all records were kept by hand.

Computers were just starting to be developed to make large-volume data-processing tasks more efficient, and Stanford was at the forefront of computer programming at that time. Of course change is never easy, and many employees and executives at City National and other banks were reluctant to adopt these new systems. But when the time came, I was way ahead of the crowd on the programming side and had a base of knowledge that proved quite useful in bringing our operations center into the modern world. That computing prowess would elevate City National and later Bank One above the pack, opening doors to all kinds of new business opportunities.

The first of many technological innovations that I witnessed was the installation of a very large and noisy machine called a magnetic ink character recognition (MICR) system. The machine could read the numbers printed at the bottom of checks in magnetic ink and sort them by account and routing numbers. Previously all the sorting was done by humans looking up the accounts by customer name.

Our MICR sorter was probably six feet tall and ten feet long, with lots of conveyor belts, mechanical arms and pockets. It directed all the checks with account numbers beginning with the number one into one pocket, the twos into another, and so on through nine. Then it would take all the individual pockets and put those checks in order. Eventually, they were all sorted and in order, ready to be returned to customers. That machine really made an infernal racket, but the thing worked.

After my stint in operations, I was assigned to credit card processing, housed in a different building on Michigan Avenue, about five or six miles from the operations center. In those days credit cards had to be reissued every year, and City National had really fallen behind. Getting this problem fixed was going to be the first real management task of my professional career.

We had machines that could stamp one new card at a time from a plastic blank. The operator would key-in a single customer's name on the keyboard, and out popped the new card. Real Stone Age stuff.

We had to get in there and automate the system so we could produce multiple cards simultaneously. This involved machinery controlled by computers running software designed for the task. Instead of producing 100 cards an hour, we were able to make 3,000 cards in an hour and run the machinery day and night until our backlog was met. Staffing of three shifts had to be managed as well. It was one of my first big management successes.

Then it was back to the operations center where I was given the responsibility of installing a new software system for customer accounts. Up to that point, if a customer had multiple accounts—say a home mortgage, auto loan, savings account and two checking accounts—everything was organized by name and address and kept in separate ledgers in separate departments. Records were literally scattered all over the place, so it was very time consuming to get a complete snapshot of all the business we did with a particular customer. And if a customer wanted to change his address, he or she had to call five different departments.

The goal was to automate all this information and organize it by name and account numbers, giving us the ability to go to the screen (a primitive cathode ray tube in those days), type in a customer's name and see all of his or her accounts and loans. It was like magic back then, and I was a boy wonder!

Why was this important? Mainly for marketing purposes. The more we knew at a glance about a customer, the easier it was to offer that person new products and services. This gave us a huge sales and marketing advantage over our competitors.

At my direction, we continued to automate all sorts of operations, eliminating ledgers and replacing them with electronic files and records. There were some bumps along the way. For example, one older colleague who ran the check processing department with probably thirty years of tenure at the bank knew nothing about data processing or computers and had no interest in learning. Zero. To get the software project done, I basically had to ignore him and work around his objections and roadblocks. It took nine long months to implement the system. When it was up and running, my borderline incompetent boss got to take all the credit, but most people at the bank knew how it got done.

In this methodical way, project by project, I had my fingers into all sorts of hidden parts of the bank that some executives had barely heard of. It really gave me a good sense of our capabilities and what it took to overcome obstacles and get things done. I was gaining confidence and was less and less worried about how people might view me as the CEO's son.

Eventually I got to run the retail branch network in Columbus, the commercial lending department, and in 1980 all the affiliate banks in Ohio. As I continued to prove myself, a funny dynamic developed. People would come to me when they wanted to get father to do something, but were too afraid or intimidated to approach him themselves. They wanted me to do it for them, and I attempted to avoid those situations at all costs.

Being the CEO's son put me in an entirely different category. Probably the hardest thing to overcome is that people are constantly judging you, making comparisons and wondering if you're a ne'er-do-well getting special treatment. Those tendencies are natural. We all do it. It's like being the starting quarterback on a football team that your father coaches. Does this kid really deserve to be quarterback?

But there were advantages. Having grown up in John G.'s household, I was familiar with his temperament from day one and accustomed to how severe a judge he could be. I also had a pretty good sense of how far I could push him before backing off. Another plus for me was that I could call him up at night and ask why he handled something a certain way. And while he might go out of the way not to chat me up or pay extra attention to me in the office, he was more than willing to spend that extra time with me in private. Those were great insights that I benefited from.

People ask if he was harder on me than on others. Absolutely. But he was hard on everybody. Father was a fair boss but very tough. My cousin Jay Hoster never worked for John G. but had this wonderful insight: "He was an amazing amalgam in that he could be this gruff businessman, but also very aware of someone's talent and skills. If you're right and you're good, you get lots of praise. But you'd better be right!"

Father not only had complete command of all the charts, graphs and tables in the annual report, he could also pluck an obscure detail from the footnotes. He could take someone into his office and totally dress him down, and then conclude, "So how's your son doing in the marching band?" and mean it sincerely. So the fear factor was offset by this sense that he genuinely cared for you.

If father was some degree harder on me, it was nothing that I couldn't take. I could deal with it because I loved him, first and foremost, and because I had so much more insight into his personality than the others did. It got to be like I was a duck, with his criticisms rolling off my back like water.

But there were moments when it stung. As I mentioned, both my grandfather and father frowned on coffee at the desk. John G., for his part, didn't think it was appropriate to have coffee stains on papers. That's fine, but the policy resulted in people taking coffee breaks away from their desks, which could be a time waster.

Lots of people wanted to change this, and at one point a delegation came to me and asked if I could help persuade John G. to change the policy. I relented, went to father, and said, "We could save a lot of time if we had coffee at our desks. Lots of people feel the same way."

Father had this way of burning a hole through your forehead with his eyes, and this was one of those moments. "Do you know who the CEO is at this bank?" he snapped.

"Yes," I answered, feeling the heat and waiting for the sonic boom.

"Good!" he bellowed. "There will be no coffee at the desks!!"

I didn't run down the hall and jump through a plate-glass window, but it was demoralizing. There were probably ten ways he could have handled the situation better, but that wasn't father's way. I learned to live with those periodic episodes, but I never really got used to them. More importantly, I was determined not to treat my subordinates in a similar fashion when I was in charge.

It was 1973, my third year at City National, and something happened suddenly to the person overseeing all the branch operations. There was an immediate opening. We probably had twenty branches in the Columbus market in those days, and the head of branches had to answer for all installment and small commercial loans up to $15,000, security and physical upkeep of branches, and oversight of all the branch employees, from tellers to managers. It was the heart and soul of the bank, a really important job.

Father thought I was qualified, but for the time being kept that to himself. He wanted other people to draw that conclusion apart from him. Uncharacteristically for him, he went to the senior managers and asked them who they thought should be running the branches. That was very much a departure from his usual top-down management style.

Several of them recommended me, but father played coy, questioning the choice and acting somewhat skeptical. Amid his reluctance, he got them to start pushing for me. I think he was clearly manipulating them—and maybe they knew he was playing a little game—but it made him feel comfortable in being asked to promote his son rather than being the first to suggest it.

Then as now, the branches accepted deposits and used that money to make loans. My job was to make sure that we took in lots of deposits and made as many loans as possible.

Each branch had loan and deposit targets, and was given an annual budget to meet those goals. But how they got there was open to interpretation. Branch managers operated like kings of tiny banking fiefdoms. They ran their branches and made their loans as they saw fit. Some were better at it than others.

If you wanted a loan for a new car or to start a small business, you made an appointment with the branch manager, came into his office and talked for an hour. There were no standard questions. If he liked you, and maybe if you had similar backgrounds and interests, you were more likely to get that loan. It was much more of an art than a science. (Credit reports were in their infancy back than and consisted of little more than local information. Spotty at best.)

After comparing each branch's performance to its budget, it was apparent that many were missing the mark. I wanted to come up with a system that was less dependent on the whims and abilities of different managers.

Common sense dictates that you can't have twenty ways of doing something and be successful as an organization. We needed a reliable way to determine 1) who should get loans (there was no Experian or TransUnion back then), and 2) standard procedures to deal with troubled loans.

I needed to get people on board, but there was one little problem: I was a numbers guy, not a credit guy. The people who had grown up in the branches and had been lenders all their life thought they *had* to be better than I because I had never made any loans.

"You'll never be a good lender until somebody talks you out of money," was how the man running our installment loan business put it to me. "You have to make some bad loans to make good loans."

So I gave it a try, working for a few months in a branch making loans. How hard can this be?

One day a guy came in seeking a loan for $12,000 to start a small business. I fell in love with what he was talking about, only to find out later that he had no intention of ever starting a business. I probably should have done more checking than I did, like calling the telephone number he gave me!

I made the loan and three months later it was charged off. The guy was a deadbeat. Not one thing he told me had been true. And everything about him that was true he had failed to mention, little details like his long history of never paying back loans. Being taken by this swindler really hurt, and it made me even more determined to come up with a numbers-based approach to eliminate the guesswork from lending.

Working with a small technology company called Fair, Isaac and Company (today called FICO Corp.), we developed a credit-scoring system for City National. Fair, Isaac was founded in 1956 by engineer William Fair and mathematician Earl Isaac. The two had met while working at the Stanford Research Institute in Menlo Park, California. Their idea was to take information, analyze it and use it to predict credit-worthiness. This was just the sort of thing I was looking for.

You'd take a large number of loans—say 15,000 loans from the previous three years—and grade the various attributes: male, female, age, salary, homeowner, renter, etc. Then you took all the variables and compared them to loans that went bad, allowing you to give each loan a credit score. Here's what it showed: If someone had a credit score over 700, one out of 100 loans would go bad. If the credit score was over 750, one out of every 200 loans would go bad. And so on. The higher the score, the less likely the loan would go bad.

Not surprisingly, our lenders hated it. Everybody said, "I've got to be there to look the customer in the eye," or, "We've always done it this way." An understandable reaction. You could just imagine them thinking, "Why should we be listening to this kid; he's just the boss's son."

My first year in implementing that new system was possibly the toughest of my career because so many of those branch managers and loan officers— many years my senior—doubted me.

To get buy-in, we gave branch managers override authority, so they could step in and say, "I'm approving this loan because it doesn't meet credit-score criteria." The result? Virtually every time they overrode the system, they were wrong. Not every loan would go bad, mind you, but fifty percent would go bad, and you don't want fifty percent of your loans going bad.

It took three long years to fully implement the credit-scoring system. I was patient, working long hours with many individuals to get them through it, as opposed to saying, "This is how we're doing this." Even if I had wanted to impose an edict, I simply didn't have the stature to throw my weight around with that crowd.

And then a funny thing happened. The system worked. Our loan portfolios were improving, with fewer troubled loans on the books. As profits increased, doubters decreased. What we proved was that the numbers were better than the loan officers. City National was one of the first banks in the country to implement a credit-scoring system in its branches, putting us ahead of our peers in profitability and loan quality.

And by the way, branch managers ended up loving the system because a portion of their pay was based on incentives. The more profitable the loan portfolio, the more money they made. Four or five years later it was like they had thought of it, not me. That experience was a real confidence builder for me.

CHAPTER NINE

Collaborative Approach

In the late 1970s, the economy was heading south. Manufacturing, the backbone of Ohio's industrial economy in those days, was feeling the pinch of rising energy prices, slack demand, high interest rates and cheap foreign competition. It was 1977 when steel mills started closing abruptly in Youngstown, Ohio, eliminating 50,000 high-paying jobs in a matter of several years, a harbinger of tougher times to come for Ohio and the U.S. manufacturing sector as a whole.

Quite separately from the steel mill closings, the man running our commercial lending department committed suicide. Beyond his personal tragedy, it's almost always a sign of wider trouble when someone in the lending business takes his or her life. It usually means, as it did in this case, that the person had made some bad loans, so the bank had problems.

The executive committee met to consider the matter. The number two person in the department was thought to be an outstanding lender but a very poor manager. So my name came up in this context. Why not John B. McCoy, who had just done such a good job implementing the credit-scoring system in the branches? I got the promotion.

The number two guy, Tom Igoe, was an extremely bright and talented commercial lender. On a scale of one-to-100, he was a ninety-nine. Everyone had great respect for his abilities. He loved my father, but he had no intention of working for me.

In fact, right around the time I started in the operations center, Tom was reputed to have stood up and declared: "There's one person that I'll never work for at this bank, and it's John B. McCoy!" So what ended up happening to Tom, with me being his boss, was a tragedy of Shakespearean proportions—for him, that is.

I decided to get an early start my first Monday morning, arriving at seven a.m., only to find Tom already there. We exchanged a brief greeting. "Hello John," "Hi Tom." Too bad, I thought, hoping to be the first one in that day to get organized, find my way around and introduce myself as people came in.

I had my own office, and right outside the door were two rows of loan-officer desks, six on each side of a large room. Tom sat on the far end of one of the rows. The first day was fairly uneventful after a series of introductions. There was no big speech delivered but I made a few remarks to the group about looking forward to working with everyone. Tom's brooding presence did cast a bit of a pall over the proceedings, but nothing that shouldn't straighten itself out if a few days, I figured.

What was eating Tom? I don't think that he ever really wanted the job, but he was convinced that I wasn't qualified to have it because of my youth

◄ *Previous page:* I held a variety of positions before being named CEO in 1984, and found success with a collaborative management approach. I still have this partners desk, designed to be used by two people.

in general and lack of experience in lending in particular. If the only qualification for the job was making commercial loans, then he was right: I wasn't qualified. But I *was* qualified to run things and let other people make commercial loans, whether Tom thought so or not.

When it was time to go home, Tom didn't budge. Just as he wanted to beat me into the office, he was equally determined to wait me out. It was his not-so-subtle way of telling me, "Kid, I was here before you and I'm going to be here after you." At eight p.m., with Tom firmly planted in his chair, I called it a day. I sometimes wonder whether he spent the night at his desk.

With the Ohio economy on the downswing, City National had an increasing number of past-due loans. The portfolio included all types of loans to car dealerships, real-estate developers, manufacturers, retail stores, health clubs, you name it. I soon discovered that City National not only had bad loans, but, worse yet, bad systems for keeping track of them. Make that no system.

As with the branch managers who made loans to retail customers, each of our commercial lenders had his own methods for following up with customers who had fallen behind in loan payments. And as with the branch managers, some were more effective than others.

My plan was to establish a department-wide process of loan review, tracking and measuring where we stood on all outstanding loans. First you assigned each loan a number between one to ten—the higher the number the better the prospects of being collected. By assigning a number, we could more easily review the loans that were in the most trouble.

We'd review the most-troubled loans in group meetings and the loan officers would discuss how they wanted to handle each situation. They couldn't just say "It's a three" one day, and come back the next week and say, "It's still a three." They had to have a plan.

The plan had to include actions, for example getting an appraisal on some delinquent buildings. If we found out that they were worth half of what we thought they were, the loan became a two. In this fashion we had current and ongoing plans for how we were going to work our way through troubled loans.

I wasn't approving credit or disapproving credit, I was simply managing how we operated the bad credits. Once again, people didn't like it because they weren't as independent anymore. But over time the economy got better and the loans got better. So that was how I got my lending experience in the business.

Computers and data processing made everything so much easier. You review and score one loan, then another, and pretty soon you have enough data for a flow chart on all the bad loans. I really didn't know that much about lending, per se, but business school had taught me a way to think about and solve any problem. It's a simple process: what is the problem, what are the various solutions and how do you find the best solution. You put these planning models and raw data together, and it worked, whether it was an operations issue or a lending issue.

People ask me why I adopted a collaborative management style. I guess the answer is part nature, part nurture.

First and foremost, it fit my personality. I was introduced to the team approach at Stanford and we could all see the benefits. Our group solutions to problems were generally superior to what we could come up with on our own. And in the military, I quickly realized that stripes or no stripes, a young squadron commander was not going to push around an old hand like Sgt. Jesse. There had to be give and take in that relationship.

And once at City National as a young executive in a traditional business environment, bulldozing my way through various assignments would have been a prescription for disaster. In 1970s corporate America, collaboration was very much an alien concept to many old timers. Tom had dug in his heels because he felt passed over and had wanted to be the leader, not part of a management team. That made perfect sense in the context of City National's autocratic, top-down leadership style.

But I was coming from a different place. Times were changing in the banking industry, and I was part of a new generation that would help usher in that change.

Would it have been easier to be a dictator? Definitely more expedient. Collaboration is slow and takes considerable patience. From a practical standpoint, I didn't have much of a choice in the matter. Because I was so young and unproven, I didn't have the stature to boss people around the way my father might have. Collaboration came naturally and felt right for me, and it worked.

I do know this: As First Banc Group and then Banc One acquired banks, our decentralized management system—keeping local management teams and giving them considerable autonomy to run things as they saw fit—fueled our growth. And in my eighteen years as CEO, a collaborative approach to management was a critical component of Bank One's success in buying and integrating other banks.

In terms of temperament and style, my father and I couldn't have been more different. Like his father before him, John G. needed to be the field general. The undisputed person in charge. The smartest person in the room. He knew every detail in an annual report or loan document, and wouldn't hesitate during a meeting to reference a particular line item or footnote to the mortification of some clueless underling. It was intimidating and sometimes humiliating.

By the early 1980s, it was clear to most observers that I was being groomed to succeed father as CEO of the holding company. It was during this time that father brought in a seasoned executive from Philadelphia National Bank, Bob Potts, to serve as president of Bank One Columbus. Father was looking for someone with credibility and connections to shore up senior management during his transition to retirement, giving me another experienced hand to call upon for advice and counsel. I believe father envisioned Potts filling the role that Ev Reese had filled for him, when he was starting out.

Potts may have had other ideas. As president of Bank One Columbus, he presided over our original banking franchise in the Columbus metro area, which was an important job that included more than just banking responsibilities. That person was our face in the community, representing Banc One the corporation in many civic ventures.

I was president of Banc One Corp., the holding company, the second-highest position in the company. Potts and all the other Ohio regional presidents (Bank One Dayton, Bank One Mansfield) reported to me, and I in turn reported to the CEO.

Looking back, I'm sure that Potts saw himself as more qualified to have my job, and also in line to run the entire corporation after father retired. He very well could have, but his skill set was not so well suited for a consumer-oriented retail bank. Potts was a skillful commercial lender, one of the best in the business, but not so experienced with the consumer products that were Banc One's bread and butter.

Because of these underlying tensions, Potts wasn't much of a mentor to me. Yet we maintained a good working relationship and he would go on to serve an extremely valuable role for Banc One when we entered the state of Texas. More on that later.

But first a quick aside. Potts and I had neighboring offices and we shared a common reception area. One summer day I was returning from lunch and noticed a man wearing gloves and sweating profusely, sitting in our reception area. He was waiting for Potts, who was still at lunch. I said hello, but when I got into my office I called Potts' secretary and said, "This is Mr. McCoy. Don't say anything, but is that man making you uncomfortable?" She said yes.

So I contacted security about a suspicious man in the building and they came storming up to the sixteenth floor, but by that time the man had left. He had asked the secretary for directions to the restroom, and she said the only one was next door at the Sheraton hotel. He was gone when security arrived. (It was very much a coincidence but Vice President Nelson Rockefeller happened to be speaking at the Sheraton that day, and when the authorities figured that out things *really* blew up. The Secret Service was called in, pretty much shutting down half the city.)

Right then the secretary's phone rang. It was Mrs. Potts, calling from home. She said she had been held hostage and had just untied herself. A man was heading downtown to meet with her husband and get the ransom money, she said.

It all started when she heard a knock on her door in a rural suburb of Columbus. The stranger told Mrs. Potts that his car had broken down and he needed to use her phone. Without waiting for a reply he pushed his way in, brandishing a gun.

Halsey Potts, who was no shrinking violet, kept her wits about her. "You're not going to shoot me, are you?" she demanded to know. The gunman stared back, seemingly pondering the question. "You're not going to rape me, are you? What would your mother think about this? What if she finds out?"

We can only guess what effect this had on the assailant, but he ultimately tied up Mrs. Potts and left her in the bathtub before speeding off toward Banc One headquarters.

For three weeks, everyone was on pins and needles, especially the Potts family. Then Potts' secretary gets a call from a man who said he'd like to meet with Mr. Potts because he had previously met his wife and wanted to discuss something with him. That set off the alarm bells.

The secretary kept her cool and wisely made the appointment. Two days later, when the hapless kidnapper arrived, police were waiting for him. Not a very wise move on that guy's part.

Less than a year later, John G. would retire (he stayed on the board as a director) and I would become CEO in addition to president. Federal and state barriers to bank acquisitions across state lines were about to fall, and Banc One was ready for its next and most explosive phase of growth.

CHAPTER TEN

Succeeding a Legend

*T*he day had finally arrived—April 24, 1984. After fourteen years of learning the ropes in increasingly senior positions, I was to be named CEO of Banc One Corp. at a board of directors meeting. It was exhilarating and emotional at the same time, getting that stamp of approval from my father and so many business leaders whom I admired and had basically watched me grow up at the bank. I wrote in my pocket planner that everything went well and that I "got teary" at the board meeting, which I don't recall any more. But I'll never forget the feeling of being entrusted with the "car keys" of a bank that began as a Model T under grandfather and, thanks to hard work and extensive retooling, had emerged as the pace car of Ohio banking.

Mentally, I was nervous but raring to go. Physically, I was a wreck. Two weeks earlier I was playing wallyball with some friends. The game is a very fast and intense version of volleyball played indoors on a racquetball or squash court. I was at the net jumping for a block when I felt a sharp pain in my leg, as if my teammate (a great guy named Frank Kass) had crashed into me from behind and taken out my legs. I hit the ground hard and wound up flat on my back looking up at Frank in pain and disbelief. "Why'd you do that?" I demanded. "Do what?" he asked. Turns out he never touched me; I'd gotten myself in this mess.

My Achilles tendon had ruptured, and it needed to be surgically repaired. In those days recovery included a hard cast above the knee. I hobbled around well enough with crutches but couldn't drive for weeks.

On the morning of the board meeting I got dressed for work as best I could. From the waist up I certainly looked the part of CEO—starched shirt, dark coat, conservative tie. From the waist down the look was entirely more casual—black sweatpants pulled tight over my cast. Perfect, I thought. In retrospect I probably looked more like a guy on his way to a costume party than someone about to be named CEO of a bank.

Columbus isn't the kind of town where executives ride to work in limos. CEOs drive themselves around like everybody else. But on this day the bank sent a jack-of-all-trades type employee to pick me up. Bright and early that morning, Jerry (I never knew his last name) pulled into my driveway. Much to my consternation he was driving a Cadillac, which was a little over the top, but to my absolute horror he was wearing one of those black chauffer's hats with a small bill in the front. I guess he thought he was just playing the part of my driver, but I didn't want anything to do with that getup. "Whoa, what's on your head?" I said in a not-too-friendly way, tumbling into the back seat. "That's the *last* thing I need." Sheepishly, Jerry removed the hat and we headed downtown to 100 E. Broad Street, Banc One headquarters.

You might be wondering what exactly I was taking the helm of. Banc One Corp. had 314 branches throughout Ohio and assets of $7.3 billion,

◄ *Previous page:* Three generations of McCoys were captured in this photograph, which was shot for the cover of *Institutional Investor* magazine after I became CEO.

up from $140 million when father started out in 1959, and 7,000 employees. While we were now the No. 2 bank holding company in Ohio in terms of assets, we remained the No. 3 bank in market share in Columbus. The heavyweights in town remained BancOhio Corp., which in 1984 was acquired by Cleveland-based National City (now part of Pittsburgh's PNC Bancorp), and Huntington Bancshares Inc., and they weren't about to roll over for us. We were gaining on them, yes, but there was plenty of work to be done and it was my job to do it.

One thing that was absolutely to my advantage was our profitability. We weren't the biggest bank in town, but we were the most profitable.

Most good banks will earn one percent on assets, which would amount to $73 million or so on assets of $7.3 billion. But father was handing me a bank that was returning closer to 1.4 percent on assets. He could have sacrificed some longer term growth and achieved earnings of $100 million in his final year, which was sort of a magic number in the banking industry because so few banks could achieve it. That would have been quite a capstone on an illustrious career. But to father's credit, he didn't push earnings for the sake of vanity in his last year.

High profits made my job a lot easier because Banc One stock was a strong currency for acquisitions. Many of the early M&A opportunities that I would pursue in Indiana and neighboring states would have been far more difficult or even impossible as a less-profitable bank. Father deserved all the credit in the world for leaving some easy profits on the table for me, so I could start from a position of strength.

Father, who was now seventy-one, kept his office on the sixteenth floor and remained on the board of directors. He attended quarterly board meetings but no longer maintained regular office hours.

When he was in Columbus, father would come to work every day. And every day at lunch time he would walk across the street to the Columbus Club, the city's most exclusive and business-oriented social club. He'd meet up with a group of guys that would go play cards at the club, something he'd never done when he worked at the bank. But when he stopped working, he'd go over there and do that. When he returned to the office, he'd bring Andes mints to all the secretaries in the executive offices.

He also started spending more time out of town, at homes in Michigan and Florida. He was pretty good at letting go, but still had a knack for needling, to keep people on their toes. He used to drive our M&A team batty when he'd say in a semi-kidding manner, "You haven't done a transaction in six months," as if to imply they were missing opportunities or somehow asleep at the switch. I didn't believe in that type of motivation, but that was part of his personality.

Even in retirement, father continued to cast a long shadow. For many months after I began as CEO the company and community remained in "tribute" mode to John G.

For example, most corporate annual reports showcase current management, with a letter from the CEO summarizing the previous year's accomplishments and outlining his or her vision for the future. A few more glossy pages covering corporate achievements and new initiatives come next, followed by the fine print and lower-quality paper of balance sheets and proxy materials.

Anyone reading Banc One Corp.'s 1983 annual report (published in 1984) would have struggled to determine who was running the company. The seventy-two-page, all glossy document was a veritable highlight reel of father's twenty-five years as CEO, starting with a quote taking up the entire cover: *"If you have the right people in the right job, and if they're motivated, you can do about anything that needs to be done."—John G. McCoy 1959–1984*

The inside cover contained a photo of father with management guru Thomas J. Peters, who also wrote a long essay about leadership and great companies for the publication. Father was listed among the pantheon of great leaders, right up there with Wal-Mart founder Sam Walton and Hewlett-Packard co-founder Bill Hewlett. A bit of hyperbole, perhaps, considering that Banc One Corp. was at that time doing business in a handful of Ohio counties!

Along the sides of several pages were photos of all thirteen members of the board of directors (excluding father but including me) with their favorite remembrances of father. "The association with John McCoy has been one of the highlights of my career," wrote Robert H. Potts. "He has been unselfish in applying his considerable energy to establishing a most enviable record of success."

Next came an account of a farewell interview in John G.'s office with a reporter from an unnamed newspaper, probably *The Columbus Dispatch* (owned at the time, ironically, by the Wolfe family, which owned a major stake in our crosstown rival BancOhio). The setting is in John G.'s office, where he and the awestruck reporter engage in a discussion about his career and management philosophy. An unseen observer describes the session as if witnessing a great encounter in history:

> "One of the critical requirements in managing innovation is to get out of the way," McCoy was saying as the reporter took hurried notes. "One of the reasons why it has been so difficult for innovation to occur in banking is because a banker's style is to have everything documented."
>
> McCoy anticipated the question forming in the reporter's mind. "It's an outgrowth of years of regulation and the fact that we must be accountable for other people's money. It's what today's textbooks call the business culture. The more everything has to be documented, the more likely it will be studied to death. So fresh ideas, the soul of innovation, don't get the chance to grow. They may get planted; but they never grow."
>
> McCoy paused to see if the point registered with the reporter. "Mr. McCoy," he finally asked, "would you explain what you mean by that?"
>
> McCoy leaned back in his chair. "The best idea is worthless until someone puts it to work..."

The reporter nodded. "Now I understand what you meant earlier when you said to be an innovative bank you have to get out of the way."

McCoy smiled and thought to himself how easy it was to describe and how difficult to do.

Asked by the reporter about the future of Banc One, father speaks of harnessing technology and the promise of interstate banking. A perfect segue to the next generation of leadership, one would think, but there is no mention of that other John McCoy (you know, the one in the cast) who is currently running the company. That would have been nice.

The annual report tribute was orchestrated by John Fisher, who greatly admired father and, after all, owed his entire career to John G.'s willingness to hire an obscure DJ as head of marketing and advertising. I'm sure no slight to me was ever intended.

Whenever an iconic leader departs a company, the successor has a mountain to climb. Imagine following in the footsteps of Sam Walton, Warren Buffett, Dave Thomas or Steve Jobs.

Yes, John G. McCoy was a tough act to follow. So here's my take on following a legend: Be gracious, be patient, be yourself. And above all, don't spend too much time looking in the rearview mirror. Go out and make some history of your own.

And that's exactly what I set out to do.

Father had absolutely laid the groundwork in Ohio, and I understood that the next frontier was beyond our borders. Fortuitously, the political and regulatory landscape was on the verge of a transformative change when I started as CEO. State banking laws that had limited the growth of financial institutions to a state, county or even a single branch were being questioned. And in times of change, there's nothing like a good crisis to build a consensus for action. The tipping point for liberalized banking laws came in the form of the Ohio savings and loan crisis of the early 1980s.

First, some terms. A savings and loan (also called a thrift) is like a bank in many ways, but typically with a more narrow focus. In those days, S&Ls were limited by law to accepting savings deposits and making mortgage, car and other personal loans to individual members. In exchange for this limited focus and emphasis on home lending, thrifts could offer 0.5 percent more in interest on savings accounts than banks could. So they had a built-in advantage in attracting deposits. Banks could live with this because we had more ways to make money—commercial loans and credit cards being two examples.

Over the years, Ohio's approximately 200 thrifts had lobbied for the right to enter new lines of business, particularly commercial lending. In effect they wanted to morph into commercial banks with the 0.5 percent interest advantage. There was some sentiment for this in the legislature and among state banking regulators, who allowed thrifts to evolve—and take on new levels of risk.

Meanwhile, extremely high interest rates imposed by the Federal Reserve in 1979 to fight inflation were squeezing S&Ls in two ways. First, the fixed-rate loans they had made at lower rates were less profitable, and secondly, they were paying more than banks to attract deposits. By the early '80s, some S&Ls that had pursued the most speculative growth strategies were technically insolvent. One of them was Cincinnati-based Home State Savings Bank, Ohio's largest privately insured thrift. (As it turns out, Home State had invested in risky government securities through a Florida brokerage, well beyond the mandate of Ohio thrifts. When those investments went bust Home State was toast.)

In March 1985, word spread that Home State was on the verge of collapse. Customers lined up for withdrawals at thirty-three Home State branches—and at other S&Ls thought to be on the ropes. To stem a potential mass withdrawal, Ohio Gov. Dick Celeste ordered the temporary closure of all seventy-one of Ohio's S&Ls whose deposits were insured by the private Ohio Deposit Guarantee Fund. (Ohio's 125 state-chartered S&Ls that were insured by the Federal Deposit Insurance Corporation were not affected.) Home State and several other thrifts did fail, quickly draining the $130 million Ohio Deposit Guarantee Fund, and leaving an estimated $4.3 billion in deposits at risk. At the time it was called the most widespread run on depository institutions since the Great Depression.

Celeste and state officials worked frantically to find a solution. One approach was to seek federal insurance for the state thrifts with private insurance. Another was to transfer the financial obligations to the state's healthy financial institutions.

Several days into the crisis, Celeste called a meeting of the state's six largest banks. He wanted us to bail out the Ohio thrifts by guaranteeing their deposits and buying their outstanding loans. The governor and Federal Reserve officials who were present were adamant that as healthy banks, we had a moral obligation to act in the interest of the customers of our competitors.

As the newest and youngest CEO in the group of six, I might have been expected to be the first to go along with a popular two-term governor and federal banking officials. But just the opposite occurred. I was more interested in what was best for Bank One's customers and shareholders. I argued at the meeting that we didn't create this problem, and there was no logic behind the banks making everyone whole at the expense of their shareholders.

"The reason these S&Ls failed is because they made bad loans," I said at the meeting. "Why would I want to buy bad loans?"

My logic may have been sound but it was not what Celeste or the Feds wanted to hear. In fact, the very next day Federal Reserve Chairman Paul Volcker called John G. to report that I was being "difficult to deal with" and would he please try to talk some sense into his son!

I discussed it with father and raised the same concerns about taking on the financial obligations of bad business decisions made by others. When we were done, he ended up calling Volcker back and saying, "I agree with my son." That was gratifying.

Without delving too deeply into the S&L crisis, let me say that the eventual solution was multi-faceted and involved the state legislature and federal regulators allowing outsiders to come into Ohio to bid on the assets of Ohio's state-insured thrifts. Chemical Bank of New York, for example, gained a foothold in Ohio by acquiring the assets of Home State and establishing a federally chartered and insured commercial bank.

In allowing out-of-state financial institutions to come into Ohio, the quid pro quo was that Ohio-based banks could also invest in financial institutions beyond our state's borders. The laws didn't change overnight and began with Indiana and other states contiguous to Ohio. Each state legislature had to approve interstate banking for it to take effect.

I didn't realize at the time that being against the governor's bailout of the S&Ls was going to open the door to interstate banking and the rapid growth of Banc One, but that's exactly what ensued. Once those barriers started to fall, the banks with the most experience in M&A had a distinct advantage.

Initially as CEO, mergers and acquisitions were not my focus. Remember that I had been president for several years with all the affiliate banks reporting to me. I had worked my way up first through operations and then lending. John G.'s long-time lieutenant Jack Havens, who retained the chairman's title after father retired, continued to take the lead in identifying and acquiring banks throughout Ohio. With Havens out making deals with Ohio banks, I could focus on overall strategy and increasing the profitability of the ones we already owned.

Why was profitability so important? That's what was going to separate us from the competition, and give our stock the high valuation that enabled us to be such prolific acquirers. Bad acquisitions can make companies less profitable, resulting in a lower stock price. The key was to buy a company and make it more profitable through efficiencies (converting two accounting departments into one, for example) and new products and services the acquired company could offer its customers. Without rising profitability, there could be no effective M&A strategy.

The way I looked at it, if the economy was growing at three or four percent a year, I wanted to grow the bank at ten percent or more a year. That was possible back then. We sometimes achieved growth of fifteen percent a year. How did we accomplish that? A big part of our success was having new products to introduce to the market—the credit card being a prime example.

By 1976 we were issuing credit cards not only for our bank, but for more than fifty others including Fifth Third and the former Cleveland Trust. Credit card processing involved anything associated with charge accounts. City National manufactured and issued the cards themselves, authorized payments for merchants, printed and mailed monthly statements to consumers, all behind the scenes on behalf of other banks. We were in the top tier of credit card processors in the country, right up there with American Express, Bank of America and Citicorp.

Our expertise in this area caught the attention of Merrill Lynch, at that time the world's leading retail stock brokerage, which was developing a groundbreaking product called the Cash Management Account. As envisioned by Merrill Lynch, the CMA would provide access to the cash in customers' brokerage accounts, either through a credit card or a check written on brokerage funds. But in those days, only banks could issue credit cards and offer checking accounts, and Merrill Lynch was not a bank.

The firm approached the leading card-issuing banks, which included City National, American Express and Citicorp. John Fisher and I were the point people on this project. After months of back and forth, one by one our major competitors passed. We said yes, however, and signed a contract with Merrill to make its CMA dream a reality.

The CMA account was introduced in 1977, and it was revolutionary in several ways. First, Merrill Lynch and other brokers had not previously paid interest on cash held in brokerage accounts, and banks didn't pay interest on cash in checking accounts, either. Merrill's new CMA did both, putting the brokerage firm in direct competition with every bank in America. This was the start of the blurring of lines that would make banks more like brokerages and vice versa. In 1981, *The New York Times* wrote that the CMA product had "propelled the firm into the leading edge of the revolution in financial services that is transforming Wall Street."

For the first time, Merrill's CMA account permitted customers to write a check or use a credit card—all handled by City National—on their margin accounts. Margin accounts were credit lines that Merrill Lynch customers could use to buy stocks on credit. At that time the margin rate was fifty percent, meaning that an individual with $20,000 worth of marginable securities in a CMA account could automatically borrow up to $10,000 against those funds.

Traditional banks were not amused. A lot of our competitors said this wasn't fair, that we were hurting our own industry to help Merrill Lynch compete with banks. John G. said the heck with it, somebody's going to do it, so we're going to do it. A number of state attorneys general, at the behest of banks, sued us to prevent this product from going forward. As a result, the CMA product didn't really start to grow and blossom until about 1980, but Merrill Lynch stuck with it, pushed it through, and made it the standard. Brokers paying interest on cash and offering check-writing privileges is the norm today, but back then what Merrill Lynch (with our help) did represented a major disruption to business as usual. Ultimately, it made us look like a real innovator too.

Another innovation was automobile leasing. Leasing is a mainstream form of financing now, but in the early 1980s we were the first bank to finance automobile leasing in a big way in Ohio. It was previously unheard of; a whole new line of business. For the first couple years we had some competition from Ford, but not from any banks—it was too unconventional. Well, we were happy to own the market. (One of our advertising gimmicks was called the "Clean Deal" loan or lease plan, through which customers got a year's worth of free car washes from the bank with a loan or lease.)

The reason customers liked the concept of leasing back then is the same as today—it significantly reduced the short-term cost of driving a new car. When you buy a car with no down payment, or a very small one, the monthly payments are going to be pretty high and last for maybe six years to pay off the loan. That's 120 months of high payments for a vehicle that will also be in need of regular maintenance—new brakes, mufflers and tires—as the years pass.

When a dealership leases a car or truck, it doesn't have to advertise the full price of the vehicle; only a piece of it—the value of the car for the length of the lease. At the end of the lease the dealer takes the vehicle back. So you can lease a vehicle for two or three years, pay a smaller monthly amount, and at the end of the lease you hand in the keys, no questions asked.

I became aware of David Legion, a forward-thinking guy in Louisville, Kentucky, who operated a private company for leasing automobiles. I was enamored with what he did and how he did it. The big issue in leasing is calculating the lease's end value. So you have to calculate, or call, what that vehicle is going to be worth three years from the start of the lease. And this guy had built a system that was remarkable on how he called the leases. The customer liked it because the payments were lower, and we didn't have any competition because no one really knew how to do it. It was a heck of a business for us.

So why did Legion want to team with us? Because he wasn't a bank. He didn't have enough cash reserves to lease as much as he wanted to. He had to borrow millions of dollars to make the leases and there was always pressure to pay that back, and limits to what he could borrow. We had the capital and he had the formula, so it was a match made in financial heaven.

We also started a construction equipment leasing business—things like front-end loaders, generators, air compressors, and jackhammers. We grew that from zero to $10 billion in loans outstanding. These were small leases, maybe $2,000 or $3,000 each, which also spread our risk and made for very predictable and profitable returns.

Banc One made a fortune on tax-anticipation loans, another product we pioneered. H&R Block brought the concept to us. They wanted to find new ways to entice customers to have their taxes prepared by H&R Block.

Let's say a customer was due a $400 federal tax refund. Rather than have the customer file the return and wait three or four weeks for the government to issue a check, we would give the person $360 on the spot (Block did this for us) and then the refund would be issued to Bank One. The fee was 10 percent of the refund, but if you look at it as a loan, the interest rate on an annualized basis was more like 60 percent. We were making a whole lot of money and it also brought us a lot of new customers who would open a checking or savings account because we were providing a service to them.

This was groundbreaking. The customer got cash on the spot and Uncle Sam mailed the refund check to us. H&R Block was happy because they got more customers for their core tax-preparation business, and we made a tidy, reliable profit on short-term loans. Instant refunds are common practice today, but it was a whiz-bang thing when we started it.

Since those days most states have imposed limits on interest that can be charged for cash-advance loans. Yes, the fees were high, but the service was voluntary and we figured we were taking a risk and could lose everything on a fraudulent tax return. Whether you agree with that type of lending or not, we were pioneers and we made a lot of money.

Another thing we were first to do was finance health club memberships. No other banks were doing it. Let's say it cost $600 to join a health club for a year. We would finance the transaction by paying the health club $300 up front and then taking on the obligation of collecting the $600. So the customer would owe us $50 a month for twelve months. (This is exactly what banks do with car loans—they pay the dealer and then collect from the buyer in monthly installments.)

About seventy percent of people would make their payments as planned. But then as now, some folks would join in January and then stop going after a few months, and stop making payments. Then it was our problem.

The bottom line was, health clubs weren't in the debt-collection business, and we were better at collecting money than they were. So they were content to take their $300 cash in hand and let us do the collecting. As with tax refunds, it was a great business for us.

Customers loved these and other Bank One products and services, and so did the banks that were looking for a potential partner. One reason small banks sell to larger banks is that they fall behind in technology and innovation and can't offer what larger banks can. All of this was part of the sales pitch we could make to banks. Join us, we're going places. In the early 1980s, no one did this better than Jack Havens.

CHAPTER ELEVEN

M&A Strategies

I was well aware and concerned about the fact that when I took over the bank, I didn't know how to do M&A. Jack had done all of the Ohio bank acquisitions before I became CEO, which as previously mentioned was about twenty-two when I took the helm. Jack had no designs on the CEO job when John G. retired. In fact, I had to beg him to stay throughout my first two years as CEO, because he wanted to retire. I absolutely needed him around at least until I could hire my own M&A specialist, something that was up near the top of my lengthy to-do list.

One day we were discussing some potential acquisitions, and I said, "Jack, what's your secret?" Jack looked at me and said, "John, what I do is I pick out the fifty banks I'd like to buy and I write each one of them a personal letter. 'Dear so-and-so, I'm Jack Havens from Bank One. We're really interested in your bank, and would love to come and sit and talk with you. We think you'll like the Bank One story. I look forward to meeting with you, and will call you next week.'"

He always emphasized in those notes that we would never attempt something on an unfriendly basis—and we never did—which made people more willing to talk to us. There was also some flattery involved, having been approached by a potential suitor.

"If I send out fifty letters," Jack continued, "I'll get eight people to say, 'Yeah, come see me,' and I'll end up buying two banks."

So that was the secret. You get on your horse and you go talk to everybody and you wait until someone says "yes." Is there anything more logical than that? It was perfect.

I always had my eye out for banking talent. And I generally heeded this advice from my father, with his usual knack for getting right to the point: "If you hire people who are smarter than you, they make you look smart," he'd say. "Don't hire dumb people because they'll make you look dumb."

Another thing John G. preached was to pay a fair price for new hires. "Don't worry if you have to pay a guy more money than you're making," he'd say, "because the pyramid always works in the end. If he's making more money than you, and he's working for you, you'll eventually start making more money." Pearls of wisdom, dispensed by a master.

William "Bill" Boardman was an up-and-coming lawyer and dealmaker for cross-town rival Huntington Bank, and a partner with the prestigious Columbus law firm now called Porter Wright Morris & Arthur. He left Porter Wright and went to work for BancOhio, which was later taken over by National City. He knew the banking business and most of the key players in Ohio. We'd see each other at business and social functions, and he also served with me and my wife Jane on nonprofit boards and things of that sort. We

◀ *Previous page:* Bill Boardman perfected the art of acquiring banks under Jack Havens and became my trusted advisor and partner in more than 100 M&A transactions.

weren't exactly friends, but we certainly were aware of one another. I thought he was the kind of rising star that a growing bank needed, and with Jack Havens itching to retire, I saw him as an heir apparent.

One day I called Bill, who is two years my senior, and asked if he wanted to run our trust department, an offer he quickly rejected as outside his area of interest. "So what is your area of interest?" I inquired.

Bill had done a fair amount of M&A work at Huntington and was cognizant of how the banking landscape was changing. Yet, up to that point his role had been confined to the final stages of deals once they had been negotiated. Bill was smart enough to realize that interstate banking was going to rewrite the rules, and he aspired to be on the front lines of deal making.

His area of interest happened to be my biggest area of need. Perfect, I thought.

"How would you like to join us and understudy with Jack Havens?" I offered. Bill was well aware of Jack, who had developed quite a reputation in Ohio banking circles. "He's going to be stepping aside and I'm going to need help with M&A."

Well, as Marlon Brando's Don Corleone character in *The Godfather* would have concluded, it was an offer Bill couldn't refuse. It also turned out to be one of the best deals I would ever negotiate as CEO.

Together, Bill and I would identify and complete more than 100 acquisitions in a little over fifteen years, taking the Bank One brand into thirteen new states and creating the largest retail-banking franchise in the country. No one can do that alone, and Bill deserves as much credit as anyone for helping to make Banc One Corp. the best in the business when it came to mergers and acquisitions.

Before Bill could run, he had to learn to walk. And there was no better role model than Jack Havens, who by October 1984, when Bill started, was in his late fifties and a veteran of nearly two dozen deals.

As vice chairman under my father, one of Jack's core responsibilities was to court county seat bankers and get them to become part of First Banc Group. He wasn't operating in a vacuum. The same strategy was being employed not only by our larger competitors in Columbus, but by even larger and better-capitalized banks in Cleveland and Cincinnati. With acquisitions limited to inside Ohio's borders, the competition was fierce.

Jack was up to the task. Outwardly, he looked every bit the part of what you'd expect a banker of his era to look like. He drove a dark brown Oldsmobile or sometimes a Ford pickup truck and was always professionally dressed in a dark suit and tie, fedora included. (He also chewed tobacco, which he would spit out in a wad when he got out of the car to make a call.) Jack had a fairly pronounced limp from an early bout with polio, which combined with his formal dress and the gravity of his visits, made for quite a grand entrance as he ambled through the front door carrying his well-traveled briefcase. All eyes were on this mysterious banker.

Jack was a master of first impressions. He was one of those folks who had a presence when he entered a room. People gravitated toward him. He was equally comfortable in the company of big-city bankers and Wall Street executives as he was with small-town bankers. He could relate to any type of person except a dishonest one. In those circumstances his face was like a venetian blind closing.

He always wore a scarlet "Block O" lapel pin in honor of The Ohio State University, his alma mater. A little chit-chat about the Buckeyes' prospects in the upcoming season or next big game never hurt in Big Ten Conference country, I can tell you that.

It was his personality that won the day. Jack had a folksy, homespun charm that played well with small-town bankers who could detect a big-city phony from a mile away. His gift was to never veer into corniness or condescension. And of course it helped that First Banc and later Banc One had a great story to tell, complete with a record of successful transactions. It never hurts to be able to tell another CEO, "Here's what we've done." A good record is so much stronger than words alone.

Jack and Bill's first trip together was a courtesy call to Belmont County National Bank in Bellaire, a small coal town in eastern Ohio across the Ohio

River from Wheeling, West Virginia, about a two hour drive east of Columbus on I-70. They had responded to one of Jack's letters of introduction. The guys set out in Jack's Oldsmobile, stopping for breakfast at a truck stop and chatting about their shared interest in agriculture and forestry along the way. "I was really curious to see what this guy would do and how he handled himself in these situations," Bill recalled.

Bellaire is not a very big or impressive place, but it's a proud community with a long history in glassmaking and transportation. The bank office was in the center of town overlooking the wide and winding river. Jack and Bill met in the boardroom with the CEO and two of his most senior directors. Banks considering a sale almost always liked to have more than one set of ears at the table. As expected, Jack did most of the talking.

The meeting followed what would become a familiar pattern. After a brief introduction and some pleasantries, they got down to business and reviewed the "book" that had previously been sent, consisting of First Banc Group annual reports, statements of philosophy and lists of other banks that had joined the fold. Not surprisingly, the conversation was more focused on culture and how the Bellaire people would be treated after an acquisition than it was about the numbers. That was generally a good omen and played to our strength—the uncommon partnership and retaining of local management and boards.

When money was the focus of merger talks, it was almost always a sign of trouble. It suggested to me that the institution's best days were behind it, or perhaps that management was selling for the wrong reasons, seeking to cash out and walk away rather than sell for a more reasonable price and be part of future success and an even greater payoff down the road. For that reason, we rarely participated in bidding wars with other banks.

Negotiations over price could be downright absurd. One time, in the final phase of acquisition talks for a midsized Kentucky bank, we were 25 cents a share apart. The CEO was working overtime for that extra quarter, which sounds trivial but would have amounted to an additional $75 million!

"I'll flip you for it," he finally said. It wasn't theatrics; he was dead serious. I was momentarily at a loss for words. I felt like a kid in the back yard vying for the right to shoot first in a game of H-O-R-S-E. "Well," I finally said, "if it were just you and me, I'd do it. But I'm not going to gamble with my shareholders' money. I couldn't do that with their money." Bill, who was also at the negotiating table, was white as a ghost awaiting my reply.

The Bellaire meeting lasted a couple of hours. After lunch, everyone exchanged the customary pleasantries and Bill and Jack said goodbye and left. Jack remarked to Bill on the ride home that he had a good feeling about this one.

As it turned out, the presentation went even better than Jack and Bill could have imagined. The CEO called the next day to say that he was very impressed with our bank and was interested in doing the transaction. Then he made an unusual request, asking if he could bring his entire board of directors to Columbus for a follow-up meeting to hear our pitch again before sealing the deal. We later found out the reason they wanted to do that was because their guys had never had lunch in a corporate dining room!

I don't remember all the details of that lunch, but I do recall that the CEO was very concerned about the fate of eight silver dollars from 1842 that were stored in the Belmont County bank's vault. "We don't know what to do with them because they've been carried on our books all these years as being worth one dollar each, but we know they're worth more than that."

I sure wish that was the toughest issue I would face as a CEO. We'd all seen deals fall apart for a variety of reasons, ranging from personality conflicts to corporate culture issues. But over eight silver dollars? That was a new one. Havens quickly put them at ease.

"We can put them on a plaque and give them to your directors as a closing present," he suggested. They liked that a lot.

The transaction wasn't especially large—the bank had assets of $125 million compared to our $8 billion or so—but it helped extend our footprint to the eastern fringes of Ohio, within spitting distance of the northern West Virginia communities that were just out of reach—for now, anyway.

For the next two years, Jack and his understudy drove and sometimes flew in a Beechcraft King Air turboprop plane all over Ohio, introducing themselves and negotiating one deal at a time. State or regional banking association meetings were also good venues for planting the flag and talking up potential partners. Wherever and whenever Ohio bankers gathered, we wanted Banc One to be represented. For Bill, who already had a law degree, those early days with Jack were like getting an M.A. in M&A.

"As a lawyer, I had never been in on those first visits," Bill said of the experience. "Those trips were a real kick. It was high-class sales. You just kept punching, and punching, and punching until you had success." Bill left our legal work to others and focused on deal making, pure and simple. I'd venture to say that most people didn't even know he had a law degree, which was a credit to him. He liked to say that when he came to the bank, he turned his diploma to the wall.

(Our long-time chief legal officer was Roman Gerber. Roman had begun his career with the FDIC in Washington, D.C., and had a wonderful knowledge and ability to guide us through the government maze of regulations that we needed for approval of the many transactions that we did. Roman served as chief legal officer for over twenty-five years and was key to our success.)

The lessons learned in Ohio would serve Banc One extremely well when we had our chance to make identical pitches in similar Indiana towns several years later. "The ability to relate to your audience is always the key," Bill said. "When you're dealing with small-town bankers, you need to be genuinely relaxed and low key. It's not like you can turn it on and off."

Moreover, honesty and truthfulness are the most important things in any type of negotiated transaction. We were always perceived to have the white hats on. We didn't do hostile deals and we weren't going to come in and fire everybody at the banks we bought.

If Jack recommended a deal, then the three of us—Jack, Bill and myself—would sit down, review the numbers, and together decide how much to offer. We didn't overpay—something even the sellers could appreciate, because 99 percent of the time they were being acquired with Banc One stock, and they knew we weren't going to overpay for the next guy either, which was good for their stock if they were long-term shareholders.

One reason Banc One was so successful in M&A was because it was a focus rather than a sideline. We made it a separate line of business—the equivalent of our branch network or commercial lending—and put Bill in charge of it. Most other banks left it up to the chief financial officer, who had lots of other responsibilities and generally lacked the focus that we had. M&A was Bill's job, period.

CHAPTER TWELVE

Indiana Opening

$\mathscr{I}$ 've previously explained how the Ohio S&L crisis of 1985 helped change opinions on the virtues of interstate banking. The second shoe to drop on the road to liberalized banking laws occurred in the same year, when the state of Indiana finally changed its laws to let its banks expand beyond county and state lines, and to let out-of-state banks come in. Ohio already had similar laws on the books, but our neighbor to the west was the first contiguous state to reciprocate. And you needed reciprocity or there could be no interstate deals. No state was going to allow foreign banks in without letting its banks make acquisitions in other states.

But there was a major difference between the two states that would come back to haunt Indiana bankers and continues to shape the state's banking industry to this day. In a word, it was experience. Indiana banks were new to

M&A, while Ohio law had given father and Ev Reese a two-decade head start in making acquisitions.

Think about it. Until 1985, Indiana banks couldn't expand beyond county lines, which not only limited the size of Hoosier State banks, but also kept their bankers in the dark about mergers and acquisitions. Indiana had three large banks in Indianapolis and a bunch of small ones everywhere else. By introducing intra-state and interstate banking in one fell swoop, Indiana legislators were putting their state banks at greater risk of being acquired because all the big Ohio banks knew how to do M&A, and theirs didn't.

The large Indiana banks would have been better served, in my opinion, if they were given a "break-in" period of intra-state banking to hone their M&A skills.

Why did Indiana wait so long to allow its own banks to expand? I think it was a numbers game. Because there were so many small banks in the state, those institutions held a tremendous amount of sway with legislators. For decades, the small banks were content with the status quo, which limited their reach but also minimized any competition they might face in their home counties.

As time passed and it became clear that large bank holding companies were the wave of the future, the small Indiana banks thought it was better to open up their markets to out-of-state banks. Why leave the field to three large Indianapolis banks when you could bring in other potential buyers, increasing competition and boosting prices for small banks?

Regardless of why or how Indiana changed its laws, the decision was a huge opportunity for us. We wasted no time in making our introductions to Indiana bankers.

By the time Indiana opened up, Jack Havens was still chairman but was no longer making the initial contact with potential targets. Bill Boardman

◄ *Previous page:* Indiana was fertile ground for M&A when the state opened its doors to out-of-state banks in the mid-1980s, and American Fletcher was our big catch, as depicted in this newspaper cartoon.

was our go-to guy for M&A, having learned the ropes in small-town Ohio. Bill would make the overtures, with or without my assistance as the situation warranted. Certain CEOs were more comfortable dealing with another CEO, so I wouldn't hesitate to take the lead if we felt those vibes.

Not long after the Indiana law changed, Bill was on the road, driving up and down the state, calling on little banks and making the case for joining Banc One. Just as he had learned from Jack, Bill always wrote in advance and asked for an appointment.

"We got to know a lot of bankers very quickly," is how he puts it.

Of course we had our eyes on the grand prize—the city of Indianapolis itself. The three largest banks in the state were all headquartered there— American Fletcher, Indiana National Bank and Merchants National Bank. Any out-of-state bank that could acquire one of these banks was going to have a real leg up on establishing a leading statewide franchise.

Within days of the law changing, Bill and I made appointments to visit each of the three Indianapolis banks. I called the head of each one, and said, "I know your law is changing, and we'd like to come and talk to you. I want you to understand how we do this. We'd like to tell you how we operate and what we do. And I want you to absolutely understand that if you have no interest in joining us after we talk, we won't bother you again."

The idea was to make the overture sound as innocuous as you could, so they would take the call. So we'd talk about what we had done, and tell them our story.

Over the years people have asked me which banks I was most interested in when entering a new market. The answer was very simple: Whichever ones would sell to us. Let me explain.

Take Indianapolis. Let's say my heart was set on American Fletcher, because I believed that was absolutely the best bank in Indianapolis, and the others were second and third best, in no particular order. And what if I only courted American Fletcher, never speaking with the others, and American Fletcher never sold to me? At some point numbers two and three would have been gobbled up by my competitors and I'd never get into Indianapolis. Bad move. The overriding goal was to acquire a top-three bank—whichever one would sell to me.

Consider what happened in Cleveland. Try as we might, we never got one of the three leading banks in that market. So we had to settle for a lot of smaller banks, and we were always weak in Cleveland.

Likewise, what if I said I'm not going to buy any Michigan banks until I get a big bank in Detroit? Then I never would have entered Michigan. The point is, you have to be opportunistic and willing to make the first big move that comes your way, even if it's your second or third choice.

What incentive did the Indianapolis banks have to sell? Obviously a chance to be acquired at a premium in exchange for Banc One stock, which was outperforming most other stocks in those days. But there was much more: We wanted those CEOs and directors to stay on board and help us build and ultimately run our Indiana operations for us. "We're not going to get rid of leadership or fire anybody. We want you to be part of the process and help us go out and buy other banks in Indiana, and then run it," I explained. A lot of people sell their company and they're gone. But a lot more care what happens to their people and communities after a sale.

On three separate days, Bill and I flew to Indianapolis to make our case to each CEO. We chose the plane for the relative anonymity it provided, as opposed to us driving around Indianapolis the way Bill and Jack had plied the streets of small-town Ohio.

We met with them all and made our case. "We're going to keep your board of directors and all your senior management," I'd explain. "We are going to do all of your data processing in Columbus, and all the accounting on our systems. So some of your accountants and some of your data processors will lose their jobs, but we can find them a place somewhere else." We promised never to do something unfriendly, and emphasized the major role we envisioned for them after any transaction.

Each one listened politely, then said something like this: "Gee, we really appreciate it, but forget it. You're never going to buy anything in our state, so bye-bye."

Were we disappointed? Sure. Surprised? Not really.

Those same executives had waited years for Indiana to permit in-state expansion. Without too much exaggeration, they all thought it was fait accompli that they would consolidate the Indiana banking system on their terms. At long last, nothing was stopping them from buying up small-town banks all over the state. Heck, they'd watched the large Ohio banks do it. How difficult could it be?

Very difficult, as it turned out.

Keen observers might have had an inkling that the task would not be a simple one. In the first two weeks after Indiana changed its laws, Bill drove around the state like an encyclopedia salesman on steroids, calling on one or two small-town banks a day. He joked that his life was like a scene from the Broadway show *The Music Man*, set in the mythical Midwest town of River City, and "Ya gotta know the territory" was a line from one of the songs that kept running through his head. "Once you know the territory, you talk the language," is something he said a lot. During his travels, Bill gleaned some interesting intelligence—chiefly that quite a few county seat bankers didn't care much for some of their Indianapolis counterparts.

Take Frank E. McKinney Jr., chairman and CEO of American Fletcher, the second-largest of the three big Indianapolis banks. Frank himself was something of a larger-than-life character, having won two Olympic gold medals in swimming in the 1960s. But Frank had an ego to match.

As CEO, he didn't just run, but tended to preside over American Fletcher. After completing a 44-story corporate headquarters, the tallest building in Indiana, Frank staked out an office on the top floor even though his employees occupied just the first nine. Now, whether intended or not, that's going to send a message to the entire workforce and beyond: "I'm way up here, and you're way down there."

Don't get me wrong, because Frank was a nice man, a good banker, and a great person to be around. But some of his imperious ways didn't play well. Advantage us.

"I heard stories from some of those bankers that when the state law changed, Frank would say, 'Hey, I've got good news for you—I've decided to buy you,'" Bill recalled. "And we would counter with, 'Here's how we've done it in Ohio. It's a template that's been around for twenty years. Here are the deals we've done; go check with these people.'" Our actions spoke louder than Frank's words.

American Fletcher's 1986 annual report is telling. "1985 marked the beginning of an exciting new era for the future of American Fletcher," Frank wrote in his "Letter to Stockholders" section. "After nearly two decades, the Indiana legislature approved a bill permitting the formation of multi-bank holding companies, liberalized cross-county banking opportunities, and ownership of banks between contiguous states. The passage of this landmark state law now allows Indiana banks the opportunity to grow, expand and compete more freely."

The letter points out that American Fletcher posted "unprecedented" net income in 1985, had purchased three Indiana banks (no mention of how small they were) and that Frank was really excited about moving into that new skyscraper ("a spectacular addition to the Indianapolis skyline.").

As for 1986, "you can be assured that American Fletcher will continue to actively seek statewide and regional banking acquisitions in key growth markets. … Our future has never looked brighter."

He was correct about the bright future, but not in the way he imagined it. Banc One wasn't sitting on the sidelines while Frank ordered furniture for the new office. We were buying Indiana banks at a rate of approximately one every month or so. Other large Ohio banks were active as well. Meanwhile, American Fletcher and the other Indianapolis banks were casting their lines and reeling in more rubber boots than fish.

Each time we acquired an Indiana bank, I'd call Frank at around four in the afternoon, after the stock market had closed for the day, and say, "Frank, I just wanted to let you know that we bought so and so, and I don't want you to be surprised tomorrow when you read it in the newspaper." And he'd say, "You son of a bitch."

In the spring of 1986, after we had acquired eight Indiana banks, Frank McKinney called me. Raising the white flag, he said, "Maybe we should talk about a deal."

I knew that was a hard call for Frank to make. For the past six months he had shown zero interest in joining us. It had to be humbling, considering that he had envisioned himself gobbling up all the small banks in Indiana to create the state's leading megabank.

"John, I'm not sure this would be the right kind of deal, and I'm not even sure it's worth your time, but some of my directors think I should talk to you," he said, earning an A for effort and a D-minus for enthusiasm.

After the call, which lasted only a couple of minutes, I sauntered into Bill Boardman's office next door to mine, and said, "Guess who just called?"

When I told him it was Frank McKinney, Bill's typically deadpan face lit up. "What did he want?" he asked.

"Well," I began. "Frank said he wasn't wild about our company but would be willing to talk. I think we've opened the lines of communication."

Frank's change of heart prompted us to shift gears. Up to that point we had kept in touch with all three Indianapolis banks. Now our focus was solely on American Fletcher.

For our first meeting, Frank suggested we rendezvous at a hotel in Cincinnati, which we did. The negotiations were very much about the dollars— what each side thought American Fletcher was worth. Because Frank owned a sizable amount of his bank's stock, he had plenty at stake.

But there was also lots of back and forth over what I'd call social stuff. Frank rightly wanted to know what his title and role was going to be. We settled on chairman and CEO of a new entity called Banc One Indiana Corp. In addition, Frank was to be named president of our main holding company, which sounded more important than it was, and he would also get a seat on the Banc One corporate board, which was a big concession on our part.

His operational role would be to run all our Indiana banks, which consisted of American Fletcher and the seven banks we had acquired or had agreed to acquire. Their names would eventually all become Bank One Indiana.

In the course of six weeks of negotiations, Frank's demeanor brightened. Yes, he had laid down his sword, but you have to give him credit for realizing that if he couldn't beat us, he should join us—on favorable terms. He was getting paid a healthy premium for his stock, and he was going to be in charge of an Indiana operation that was larger than what he currently had.

Before any negotiated deal is announced to the public, most companies want both boards of directors to have approved the transaction. Contracts are drawn up specifying terms and committing both sides to the deal. There are always escape clauses, but a simple change of heart or failure to conclude a deal in a timely fashion is not only an embarrassment, but will cost the deficient party dearly in breakup penalties.

By July 1986, the American Fletcher deal was signed and sealed, but not quite delivered. Frank and I both traveled to New York for the announcement of the deal at the opulent Waldorf Astoria hotel. New York was a frequent venue for such events because of the proximity of Wall Street analysts and the financial media, and being on neutral ground was always more comfortable for the executive of the company being acquired.

When everyone had arrived in New York (each bank had its own private plane for travel) and checked into the hotel, the deal was announced on a weekday afternoon, after the financial markets had closed. Our press conference to go over all the details was scheduled for the following morning at 9 a.m.

That night, the two sides got together in the hotel for drinks. The mood was festive and we could all relax and get to know each other on a personal level after weeks of intense negotiations. Our head of investor relations, George Meiling, was a big swimming buff and was simply fascinated by the fact that Frank had won two Olympic gold medals. You'd never have known that Frank had accomplished the feat, because he never spoke about it or displayed his medals in his office.

There we were in the hotel lobby, feeling pretty good about our deal and having drinks, and George got Frank to reminisce a little. Frank was opening up about the training and the competition itself, and it made me feel really good about how the two sides were bonding.

The next morning we held our press conference, attended mainly by banking analysts. As it progressed it was clear that they were very interested in what I was saying while virtually ignoring Frank. That's to be expected in these types of transactions—the buyer always gets more attention than the seller.

When it was over, Frank and I climbed into a limo to drive out to a small airport in Teterboro, New Jersey, where our respective planes were waiting. I remember feeling great, but Frank didn't say much. When we got to the airport, Frank approached me on the tarmac and said, "I've been thinking a lot about this transaction and I've decided I don't want to go through with it. I have a lot more experience than you and I really should be running the whole thing."

Here we had just announced our deal to the world at the Waldorf Astoria in New York, and now Frank was having a temper tantrum. Someone please pinch me because I'm dreaming, I thought, or get me to the nearest emergency room because I'm having a stroke and nothing is making sense.

"Frank, the deal is done," was all I could think to say. "We've got to find a way to work together."

Frank was miffed about being an afterthought at the press conference. The deal wasn't really about him or American Fletcher, and that realization was extremely difficult.

Fortunately, Bill Boardman and Jack Havens were present. Havens, the master negotiator and smoother of ruffled feathers, had grown close to Frank, and was able to convince him—right there on the tarmac—that it would be a disaster to back out now. Crisis averted.

Banc One officially acquired American Fletcher on January 26, 1987, for Banc One stock valued at $552 million, adding $4.1 billion in assets to our $11 billion, and eighty-three branches primarily in the Indianapolis area. Frank got to sit atop his skyscraper, presiding over the state's largest bank after all. Only the name on the building was Bank One rather than American Fletcher.

Once Fletcher was in our hands, the other large Indianapolis banks were not long for this world. In 1992, NBD Bancorp of Detroit bought Indiana National Bank, and a year later National City acquired Merchants National. Just like that, Indiana was left without a major financial institution headquartered in the state. To this day, the largest bank based in Indiana (Evansville-based Old National Bancorp) is about the size of Banc One way back in 1986.

I tell this story not to gloat but to illustrate just how fast the banking landscape was changing and to underscore that the banks with the most M&A experience had a significant advantage over their peers who did not. The Indiana banks were sitting ducks and the big ones got picked off incredibly fast.

Our acquisition of American Fletcher was the largest in our history and among the ten-largest interstate banking deals in the country up to that time. With combined assets of $17.4 billion (adding in pending acquisitions of both banks), Banc One was now the largest bank in Indiana and second-largest in Ohio.

"I've been waiting for something like this to happen," one financial analyst told *American Banker*. And boy, were we glad it was us.

Wall Street greeted the deal enthusiastically, though some observers questioned the premium we paid for American Fletcher—roughly fifteen times the company's prior-year earnings and more than two times its book value, which was quite a lot. Paying too much for an acquisition can harm you in two ways—by making future acquisitions more expensive if you dilute the value of your stock, which is your currency in M&A; and by making you vulnerable to a takeover if your stock becomes too devalued.

But because we were one of the most profitable banks in the country and our stock traded at a multiple of 2.5 times our book value, we could afford to pay a premium for a market leader like American Fletcher. (Book value is roughly a bank's net worth, or assets minus liabilities. Banks that are doing poorly or in undesirable markets sometimes sell for *less* than book value.)

"They've got a stock that's so powerful they're crazy not to use it," one investment banker told *The Wall Street Journal.*

Our goal was to become the preeminent bank in the Midwest, and our rapid rise in Indiana was a great start. It really got the attention of our industry and the investment community, signaling that Banc One was going to be a player. It made us look different from all the other Ohio banks, which were among the most active in the region.

Indiana turned out to be a great market for Banc One. Frank was the titular head of things, but we quickly realized that his second-in-command, Joe Barnett, was a better operator and the person we could count on to oversee day-to-day activities. Aside from monthly management meetings, which in those days were held in Columbus, Frank was largely out of the picture.

One time Frank suggested that we hold the monthly session in Indianapolis, and if we did so, he would invite a special guest for a presentation.

As an alum and prominent business leader, Frank sponsored the weekly radio show of Indiana Hoosiers head basketball coach Bobby Knight, one of the most successful and controversial college coaches of all time. Knight has a big following in Columbus because he was not only our Big Ten nemesis but also a former college player at Ohio State. Frank had asked Knight if he would address our management group, and the fiery coach had agreed. Sort of.

Frankly, I couldn't have cared less about hearing Bobby Knight, but I liked the idea that we would all come to Indiana as a show of appreciation and inclusion for our new colleagues there. When the day arrived, all the top managers from headquarters got in a plane and headed west, with talk of Bobby Knight literally in the air.

At about 3 p.m. with the meeting underway, Frank turned to me and said, "You know, Bobby is supposed to be here at six o'clock, but if he has a bad practice, he's not gonna come."

"Frank, are you kidding?" I said, incredulously. "We've got all these people over here, if he has a bad practice then he's not gonna come?"

"That's just the way he is," Frank replied. "You should have known that."

Now I was ready to do my best impersonation of Coach Knight and throw a chair across the room.

"Frank, if you had told me that he might not come, we would never have done this thing here." The meeting continued.

Promptly at 6 p.m., the door flew open with a boom, and Bobby Knight was there in his trademark red sweater. "My goodness it's great to be here, Frank's done everything for me, you guys are the best," and on and on. Knight speaks in run-on sentences with no paragraphs, using up all the oxygen in the room, the result of which can put his audience in a trance.

After fifteen minutes, he was winding down. "This has been great, I really appreciate it," he told us. "Look, I'm gonna take questions, but the first dumb question and I'm out of here."

Nervous silence. The first dumb question? Who in their right mind would risk such a thing? That unlucky slug would forever be known as the dummy who asked the worst question ever and sent Bobby Knight packing. We looked at each other, and Knight looked back, eyebrows raised.

My mind raced. No one was asking a question, and I was the leader of this group. I'm going to have to ask the first question, I thought. What in the blazes was I going to ask Bobby Knight?

Suddenly, a hand shot up. Knight saw it right away.

"Yes sir!" he shouted, pointing to Tommy Rice, the owner of the hand.

"Mr. Knight," Tommy began in a calm voice. We were all holding our breath. "When you are having a real problem, who are the three people you would call."

Bobby Knight blinked several times, as if in disbelief. Oh boy, where's my briefcase, I thought to myself.

The coach rubbed one hand across his chin in contemplation, then leaned toward Tommy, and said: "That's really good."

Yessss! Everyone exhaled and smiled. What a great question!

Knight answered the question (former University of California basketball coach Pete Newell, Fred Taylor, Knight's former college coach at Ohio State, and Henry "Hank" Iba, former college basketball coach and Olympic gold medalist as a coach) and proceeded to field a bunch more and stay for dinner. He made us feel like the greatest group of people he'd ever been associated with. Frank was beaming like the father of the bride at a wedding reception, and rightly so. It was perfect.

With Indiana in the Banc One fold, Bill and our M&A team turned their attention elsewhere, soliciting and acquiring banks in Kentucky, Michigan, West Virginia and Wisconsin. Interestingly, more banks were seeking us out as an acquirer of choice. I'm sure it was our reputation for only doing friendly deals and for keeping local management and boards in place. We clearly had a winning formula.

For example, A. Stevens Miles, CEO of Louisville-based First Kentucky National Corp., approached me around this time about a possible combination. First Kentucky was the state's largest bank, and we hadn't purchased anything of size in the state. He called me up one day and said he'd like to meet with me, but not in Louisville.

"Great, I'll tell you what I'll do," I said. "I can fly into Lexington, and there's this motel at the airport. I'll get a room." Agreed.

So I flew to Lexington and checked into the motel around 3 p.m. I'd never stayed there before, and it turned out to be quite a bit seedier than I had anticipated.

A half hour later, Miles arrives. He looked shocked entering the dingy room, with its lone twin bed and single chair. The guy is big—about 6-feet 5-inches—so I offer him the chair and I took the bed. Have you ever negotiated a bank deal sitting on a bed? I don't recommend it. We had a good laugh over our accommodations.

The next time we met I rented a bus owned by Wendy's founder Dave Thomas, who was from my hometown of Columbus. (Way back in the day father had loaned Thomas money to open his first Wendy's restaurant, a few blocks from our bank's headquarters.) Once again I flew to Lexington, but this time the bus met me at the airport, and then we picked up Miles. This time we negotiated "Dave's way"—on his bus—which was much more comfortable than the motel, I can assure you.

Ultimately, we didn't strike a deal with First Kentucky—National City bought them for $660 million in 1988. We ended up buying the third-largest bank in Kentucky. I never held a grudge against Miles or Dave Thomas, but I haven't rented a room in that motel since!

How we ended up in Wisconsin is another example of our growing reputation within the industry. In June 1987, the state's third-largest bank, Marine Corp., got an unsolicited offer from Marshall & Ilsley Corp., Wisconsin's second-largest bank. (First Wisconsin Corp. was number one.) Since both banks were headquartered in Milwaukee and there was significant overlap in personnel and branches, the combination would have resulted in massive layoffs and other cost-cutting for it to make financial sense.

Marine's CEO, George Slater, called me out of the blue. We had never met but of course we were aware of one another. He also knew how we did transactions, so that's why he was calling me and not National City or somebody else.

"Hi John," he began. "We've got an interesting thing going on, and I'm wondering whether you and I can have a conversation."

That was typical of these kinds of calls. Most executives wouldn't come out and say, "We've got a bank trying to take us over—help!" He was probably being coached by an investment bank that he had hired to advise him on the hostile bid. These were both public companies and there are rules about the timely disclosure of material events. The idea would be to come across as strong and in control, not weak and under siege, and to basically start a dialogue. Of course I could read between the lines, but in that first call you want to respect the other person's sensitive position and keep things general.

Time was of the essence. We put together a due diligence team to study the operations and financial condition of Marine, and a week later everyone flew to Wisconsin to meet with Slater and his team in the historic and quite opulent Pfister Hotel in Milwaukee.

Wisconsin had just recently relaxed its banking laws to allow in-state branching and out-of-state acquisitions. Marine had gone on a buying spree, purchasing banks throughout Wisconsin, in addition to those in Minnesota and Illinois, including Chicago. Then M&I came calling. By the time Slater approached me, Marine consisted of twenty-one banks with seventy-six offices.

Within a month, we had negotiated a $543 million deal for Banc One to acquire Marine, adding $4.2 billion in assets to our existing $18 billion. Since Minnesota and Illinois didn't allow bank ownership by companies based in Ohio, Marine had to sell its branches there. After the deal closed, Banc One consisted of fifty-seven banks with 546 offices in Ohio, Indiana, Kentucky, Michigan and Wisconsin. (Illinois finally approved interstate banking in December 1990, and we were able to buy back what Marine had sold.)

We didn't share a common border with Wisconsin, making it the first time we had entered a non-contiguous state. Conventional wisdom says it's best to expand into contiguous territory, methodically building your brand in concentric circles rather than random leaps and bounds. But why not Milwaukee? The deal had appeared unexpectedly, and we felt that if Indianapolis made sense for us why wouldn't we want to be in Milwaukee. The answer was, it did make sense. So what if we had to leapfrog a couple of states to get there.

Slater ended up as chairman and CEO of Bank One Wisconsin, and he became vice chairman and a director of Banc One Corp. There were no mass layoffs at Bank One Wisconsin and their former board of directors stayed intact and continued to direct state operations. It was a far better fate than what awaited Slater, his board, management team and employees at the hands of their cross-town rival.

"We are very disappointed," M&I Chairman J. A. Puelicher was quoted in the paper after learning of Marine's decision to sell to us. And you can't blame him for feeling that way.

CHAPTER THIRTEEN

Dial 'M' for Texas

In 1989, opportunity came knocking once again, complements of another financial crisis even worse than the Ohio S&L mess of several years earlier. But this time it wasn't in our backyard, or even in our region.

Texas, the land of oil barons and cattle rustlers, is a classic boom-and-bust state if ever there was one. And the late '80s were one big bust.

In March 1988, the largest bank in Texas, Dallas-based First Republic Bank, entered FDIC receivership after filing bankruptcy, becoming the largest U.S. bank failure in history. The FDIC took over the bank, put up $3.9 billion to cover anticipated losses, and quickly set out to find a buyer.

This was a real crisis. First Republic was the fourteenth largest bank holding company in the country and the largest bank in the Southwest. It had one-third of all deposits in Dallas and nearly as much in Austin, and a strong franchise in other major Texas markets. First Republic fell victim to declines in the energy market and subsequent weakness in real estate and agriculture. With the agency seizing control of the bank, FDIC member institutions were on the hook.

Who wants to buy a failed bank? Maybe another regional competitor looking to gain market share in an existing market, or perhaps an opportunistic bank in another region looking to expand its footprint. In recent times, private equity firms or similar investment groups have sought to buy troubled banks at a fraction of their value on favorable terms, hoping for a quick turnaround and eventual sale at a profit. The key is to understand the risks—primarily in the failed bank's loan portfolio—and price the troubled assets accordingly. This can be difficult to do in a bidding process with a short timeline.

Out-of-state bank holding companies normally would not have been eligible to acquire a Texas bank at that time, but the FDIC had override authority in a crisis. Banks from around the country were encouraged to enter the process. Bidders included Citicorp, Wells Fargo and Charlotte-based North Carolina National Bank (NCNB). We kept an eye on the process but decided not to enter. This was pretty far afield for us geographically, and possibly a financial stretch given that First Republic had assets of $33.4 billion to our $25 million or so.

I felt that Citicorp, a well-capitalized money-center bank, was the odds-on favorite to get it, but as it turned out, NCNB (later called NationsBank and currently Bank of America) emerged the winner. I thought, "Oh my goodness, this is going to be the greatest screw-up of all time." But it turned out to be probably the best bank transaction I'd ever seen.

Why? The government was desperate for the deal to succeed so they structured a sale that really had no risk for NCNB. From an acquirer's standpoint, it was beautiful.

◄ *Previous page:* Our acquisition of MCorp in Texas was Banc One's first foray outside the Midwest and investing legend Warren Buffett was among the first to find out. The MCorp deal really put us on the map as a buyer of choice in the industry.

The FDIC set up two banks—a "good" bank and a "bad" bank. NCNB had up to two years to decide which loans went into the good bank and which went into the bad bank. For the loans that went into the bad bank the government took all the losses with NCNB managing those loans for a fee. NCNB had full responsibility for the loans that went into the good bank.

It's rare, in a failed bank situation, for the FDIC to give a buyer so much time to assess the value of loans and to decide which ones to keep. Generally the bidder has to come up with a price for the entire loan portfolio—good loans and bad—in a very short time frame. NCNB also was the beneficiary of tax write-offs valued at $1 billion that sweetened the deal considerably. NCNB's future earnings in Texas would be sheltered with losses that were accumulated by First Republic. In other words, NCNB would not have to pay taxes on its Texas profits for years to come. (This tax provision turned out to be very controversial and led to changes that limited so-called carry forward losses in the future.)

The terms were so generous that an idiot should have taken the deal. The more we studied its structure, the more we admired it. We felt we had missed a golden opportunity, as did everyone else who had participated in the deal. In banking, hindsight can be a good thing, if you understand what happened, learn from your mistakes so you don't repeat them.

The First Republic transaction got us thinking more about Texas. Here you had the nation's fastest-growing state with seventeen million people and $150 billion in deposits up for grabs. Sure, there was risk, but with risk comes reward.

There were lots of small banks failing in Texas, and Bill and I discussed whether it made sense to pursue a strategy of buying up a bunch and combining them. The piecemeal approach is not the easiest way to enter a new state, but it can be done.

We explored the strategy with a friend of mine who was in the Texas banking business. Ron Steinhart and his investor group were creating a bank holding company in Dallas called Team Bancshares and acquiring failed banks. Bill and I met several times with Ron but ultimately decided not to take part. (We did end up acquiring Team in 1992 for $782 million after it had amassed assets of $5.5 billion, and Ron became chairman of our Texas operations.) But in 1988, we concluded that we could not start from zero and buy enough small Texas banks to be competitive.

In the spring of 1989, the second-largest bank holding company in Texas could no longer keep its head above water. After losing $903 million the previous year, Dallas-based MCorp was declared insolvent by the FDIC. The government had to put up $2 billion to rescue yet another Texas bank holding company, this one with $18 billion in assets.

MCorp had only five profitable banks, which regulators left alone, leaving twenty failed banks with assets of $13 billion that were stripped out and combined into the newly created, government-owned Deposit Insurance Bridge Bank. A buyer would be sought.

Bill didn't want to miss out on another chance to purchase distressed assets from the government and extend our brand into the south. "I think we ought to bid," he said to me. We both knew that nobody would get as good a deal as NCNB because the government said they weren't going to make the terms as attractive. "I still think it's an opportunity," Bill concluded, and I agreed. When you're going in a new direction people are always nervous. But I found out over time that the first guy who does a groundbreaking transaction gets the best terms. The first deal is usually the best deal.

The way the bidding process worked was that first you had to submit a bid, and then you got to do due diligence—poring over the books and talking to key employees in the brief window available. The whole process was supposed to be confidential, with only the government knowing the identity of all the bidders. (One reason things are kept confidential is in case there are no other bidders, to ensure that the government gets value from the sole bidder. Secondly, bidders don't necessarily want the investment community to know an offer is in the works, because companies making acquisitions generally see a near-term decline in their stock price. Finally, very few companies want their competitors to know what M&A strategies are being pursued.)

When we told the FDIC that we wanted to bid, we sensed some skepticism. In general, I don't think they thought we were big enough to pull it off. In addition, this was our first attempt to purchase a bank with troubled assets, which only added to our long-shot status. While some banks grow almost exclusively by acquiring their failed competitors, this had never been our style. We had lots of experience in buying good performers and making them great performers, but we were admittedly neophytes with bringing banks back from the dead.

As far as I was concerned, capital was king. A lot of companies would operate with minimal levels of capital and when they wanted to do a deal they needed to raise funds. We always maintained excess capital, which cost us money. But by having the excess capital, when the next deal came along, we were able to outmaneuver some of our competitors who couldn't get into the bidding because of their lack of funds. We were willing to sacrifice some near-term profits for the ability to move quickly on a deal.

We assembled a team of about twenty people, led by Bill and another of our executives, Don McWhorter, to go to Texas to prepare our bid. They spent the better part of two weeks in Texas reviewing the individual banks and all the problem loans.

In situations like this, it's up to the FDIC to keep all the bidders away from each other and the entire process confidential. There were rumors about who was down there, but since we were all in different locations, no one knew for sure. We did determine that the private-equity firm KKR was preparing a bid, as was Wells Fargo. (Wells took a look but ended up not submitting a bid.)

We were assigned temporary space in an office building several blocks from MCorp's headquarters. We later discovered that some of our competitors were much closer to the bank office and its records than we were, leading us to believe that the government didn't think we were serious bidders. It's funny how you read into such minor signals, but in my experience the little things often carry outsized weight.

Shortly after we arrived, Bill and Don did something that was typical of Banc One but strange as heck in the eyes of the FDIC. They told the regulators that they wanted to visit all twenty banks within the holding company and meet the top three people at each one.

"The FDIC officials said, 'That's a big job, why do you want to do that?'" Bill recalled. "And we said because we're very concerned about management. We have an operating model that requires good local management, so we want to go touch and feel these banks and talk to all these people." I'll bet we looked like serious bidders at that point!

So Bill and Don did their best impersonation of Bill and Jack Havens five years earlier in small-town Ohio, but this time flying around Texas to visit twenty banks in a week. The local officers were definitely surprised at all the attention, but happy to share their knowledge about local market conditions and loan portfolios. I think that they were flattered that we paid those visits, but flattery would get us nowhere with the FDIC. It was all about the offer.

After dozens of individual meetings, our people determined that while there were some very bad commercial loans in the outlying regions, most of the big problems were in Dallas. For example, one manager in Waco "spilled his guts," in Bills words, telling us he was forced to put bad loans from Dallas on his books, though his lenders had nothing to do with them.

We came to the conclusion that there was a core of good managers at MCorp, possibly let down by senior management in Dallas. (The head of MCorp's San Antonio bank, Bob Davis, would eventually run Bank One Columbus and later became CEO of USAA.)

Thanks to those visits and interviews, we felt we had a competitive advantage over the other bidders. Though still a considerable risk in a faraway land, the MCorp remains held great promise. Or so we hoped.

All the bidders were flying blind to a great extent. The MCorp process was a financial rummage sale in which you had to bid on and buy everything. Here's how FDIC Chairman L. William (Bill) Seidman, in his 1993 memoir, described his role and the financial mess of 1985-91, when rising interest rates and bad real-estate loans triggered thousands of bank and thrift failures:

"(My) job combined all the best aspects of an undertaker, an IRS agent and a garbage collector. Each (failed institution) arrived with records in disarray, key personnel gone, lawsuits by the hundreds and a management that was still mismanaging or had departed and left the cupboard bare."

And that's what we were hoping to buy.

After the bids were submitted (the parties remained confidential), media reports and our industry sources were pointing to two finalists: KKR and us. If true, we felt good about our chances. Buyout firms are short-term investors who generally buy troubled or underperforming companies, install new management, improve efficiency and profitability, and then sell to someone else or take the company public as quickly as possible at a large profit. They exit very fast because their game is to buy and sell companies, not run them. They have investors and lenders to pay off, and their capital is short term and expensive. We told the FDIC that unlike KKR, we weren't going to flip MCorp after a few years. We'd be there for the long haul.

Several weeks passed until the FDIC told bidders to expect an answer at 1 p.m. EST on an upcoming Tuesday. I put it on my calendar. At the designated time, I was seated in my Columbus office with Bill and Don awaiting a call from the FDIC's Seidman. It didn't come.

"It means we're not gonna get it," I told the guys dejectedly. "No, it means we're still in it," Bill insisted.

We just sat there looking at one another and out the window at the Ohio Statehouse. This was before the smartphone era, or we would have been checking our email to pass the time. Come to think of it, we probably didn't have email back then. (Funny aside: Around 1997 computers and email were being accepted by corporate America, and I thought it was a good way to communicate. We bought every senior manager an IBM laptop, which cost about $1,000 back then, so they could have email. They had to spend two Saturday mornings in computer school in return. Everyone got an email address but nobody was using it. So at the end of the year, when it was time to award bonuses, I sent everyone an email with the bonus figures for their groups. Nobody saw them. Finally one guy checked his email and all the other managers came rushing to me to get their figures. I said check your email, and that's how they started using it.)

Two o'clock came and went, and so did three o'clock. Now we were concerned. Four o'clock and nothing has happened, and we're climbing the walls. What's going on here? At 5:30 I was supposed to fly to Omaha to have dinner with Warren Buffett (we were friendly and would meet once a year for dinner), and now I was really frustrated because I hadn't heard anything and I didn't want to miss my dinner with Buffett. I told Bill and Don I was leaving for Omaha because we weren't going to get this thing, and off I went. They waited in the office for the call to come.

I flew to Omaha in our corporate jet, calling my office every fifteen minutes from the awful phone on the plane, which was really more like a radio. No word from the FDIC, they said. In Omaha, I took a taxi from the airport to one of Buffett's favorite spots, Gorat's Steak House. The local time was 6 p.m., an hour behind Columbus, and still no call.

The restaurant was very nice and smelled like steak heaven. Buffett was waiting for me at a corner booth, drinking his trademark Cherry Coke. After some brief pleasantries, I told the world's greatest investor that I had been waiting all day for an important call, and if it came during dinner I'd have to take it. No problem, he said, ordering his customary T-bone steak, cooked rare, with a double order of hash browns. I asked for a filet with french fries, and most likely a gin. Maybe a double.

About a half hour later, my phone rings (we did have crude cell phones then). It's Seidman. He called my office first and my secretary, Laura Gray, gave him the number.

"John, this is Bill Seidman. Where the hell are you, I told you to be in your office," he began. I motioned to Buffet that this was the call and stepped away from the table.

"Bill, you told me to be in my office at one o'clock, and now it's 7:30," I protested. "I was scheduled to have dinner with Warren Buffett, and I'm here in Omaha having dinner with Warren."

"Oh, give Warren my best, he's one of the best guys in the world!" he shouted.

"And by the way, you got the deal. We're going to announce it at eight o'clock tomorrow morning in Washington, and you have to be in Texas for your announcement. Nice going, John."

It's funny how life works sometimes.

I returned to the table, and Buffett could sense something was up. Because the markets were closed and the deal would be announced before they opened again, I shared the exciting news. He was thrilled for me, and said to let him know if we needed any financing for the deal. "I'd be happy to take a look at it," he said. (A few weeks later, I thought that the market would see it as a positive if Buffett participated in the deal. I went back and visited with him, and he went over the terms. I said, "Warren, I appreciate your willingness but those terms are way too expensive for us. We think we've got enough capital anyway, and he said, smiling, 'I know you do.'")

After dinner I flew back to Columbus, heading directly home. It was hard to sleep. I needed to be back at the airport for the 6 a.m. flight to Dallas. We had a small office in the private hanger at Port Columbus International, where we kept our plane. When Bill and the others began arriving the next morning, we were all smiles, high-fiving and back-slapping one another. Joining us were Don, George Meiling our treasurer and Tom Hoaglin, chairman and CEO of Bank One Dayton. Tom, who joined the bank in the banking officer program that John G. had set up to hire MBAs, was going to be running the Texas banks for us.

During the two-hour flight to Dallas we talked in general terms about what it would take to incorporate the former MCorp operations and employees into the Bank One system, and who would say what at MCorp headquarters. We had a big day planned.

Siedman made the announcement from Washington while we were still on the plane. Our press release announcing the deal was distributed simultaneously. We called the office from the plane a couple of times to see what the reaction was in the media and on Wall Street, and early indications were favorable.

In Texas, we were greeted at Love Field by Jim Gardner, the most senior official left at MCorp who hadn't been kicked out by the Feds (the bank was technically called Bridge Bank at that time). He was there to drive us to MCorp headquarters. Bill and Don had been to the office before, during the bidding process, but this would be my first visit.

"I really appreciate you picking us up," I told him once we were in the car.

"You're welcome," he said, then looking over, added: "I quit."

"You quit?" I said in disbelief. "You can't quit." Heck, at this point we couldn't have found the restrooms in our new Texas office without this guy.

"Well, you didn't offer me a job, so I figured I was out," he explained.

I told him we hadn't offered anybody a job, due to FDIC bidding rules that kept us from doing exactly that.

"Well, the other people offered me jobs," he noted, which really steamed me.

We were able to convince the guy to stay, and I think he appreciated that we had played by the rules.

There's a saying in our business that when a bank builds a new headquarters, it's ready to fail. That's exactly what played out at MCorp. The bank's main offices were in a recently constructed 55-story granite and glass building known as the "Keyhole Building," a reference to a six-story hole in the center of the building near the curved-glass top. Inside, it had an open atrium from the basement to the sixth floor. The bank's trading floor was housed in the basement, and the first floor had walkways over the trading floor, allowing you to look down on those operations.

The bottom third of the building was occupied by MCorp employees. We were scheduled to greet them from a podium erected in the middle of the main walkway. The workers came out of their offices and were looking down over glass railings into the atrium below. It was a dramatic setting.

After months of uncertainty and the ultimate failure of their company, those several thousand MCorp workers who still had jobs were curious as heck to know who their new employer was. Well, it was me, and everyone was taking their first look.

Given the coliseum-like setting, it was tempting to open with, "Friends, Romans, countrymen, lend me your ears," which I resisted. "We're excited about this transaction, and we're excited about the people we've met so far," I began, speaking off the cuff. "We think there's a great opportunity for your future to stay with this bank."

I ran through some of our previous transactions and explained how we did them, and what they could expect as Banc One employees. We were depending on each one of them, I explained, to help make this transaction successful.

After about ten minutes I was nearing the end of my remarks. I wanted them to know that even though their bank had failed, they were not failures. That they fought the good fight, and didn't win because they couldn't win.

"I believe you failed because of the economy of Texas. If I had been running the bank, we'd be in the same fix as you are today. The fact that your bank failed was because they were all going to fail. Now what we have to do is fix it."

I got a big ovation, and why not? They had hope. While Banc One was virtually unknown in Texas, our company had two things going for it from the outset: We were not a Texas bank, which would have meant the elimination of a bunch of jobs to make the acquisition work, and we had a well-earned reputation for taking care of the people we acquired. In business and many other pursuits, actions do speak louder than words.

We wouldn't take over the bank for another thirty days. We sent bank presidents and other senior people to Texas to answer questions and meet with their people. Over the next month I visited every bank in the state that we owned. Our people did a great job making our new Texas employees feel like an important part of the family, which they were.

Tom Hoaglin, who had done a great job for us as chairman of Bank One Dayton, was superb as chairman of Bank One Texas. He had to build a senior management team from scratch, because the FDIC had taken out the top ten people from MCorp, banning them from working for Banc One.

After I addressed MCorp employees, I visited the office of the former CEO of MCorp, Gene Bishop. He remained in charge of an MCorp holding company consisting of five Texas banks that had not failed. I was looking for any insights I could get.

Bishop was pleased that I came and saw him, but you could just tell how disappointed he was for having presided over such a colossal bank failure. He told me all the people I should go see in town. One thing he felt strongly about was that we should hire a Texan to run Bank One Texas. He suggested Harvey Mitchell, a long-time Texas banker turned oilman. I tracked him down and made him an offer to come in as Tom's right-hand man.

"I'll only take the job if I'm the CEO," said Mitchell, a cigar-chomping, back-slapping guy who seemed to know everyone in Dallas. Tom, to his credit, felt that they could get along and said it was OK if Mitchell got to be chairman and CEO. Tom was named president. That was a pretty good thing Tom did, and they were an effective team.

We had beaten out not just KKR, but also NCNB, First City Bancorp of Texas, Chemical Bank's Texas Commerce Bancshares unit and the Bank of Scotland. The deal was complex, but in simplest terms we had agreed to put up about $500 million over several years for MCorp. We paid the money to the FDIC which in turn used it to capitalize the twenty MCorp banks that previously had no net worth. So in that sense the money came right back to us.

As it had with First Republic, the FDIC created a good bank and a bad bank for MCorp. We got the good bank, which consisted of all performing loans that we had selected, sixty-three branches and other MCorp offices in twenty-nine Texas cities and towns, and 5,500 new employees.

In addition, we agreed to run a separate company to collect the bad loans on behalf of the FDIC. We didn't have any of the risk of the bad loans, but we would get twenty-five percent of anything we collected. We ended up earning $45 million a year of non-interest income out of that activity. Collecting bad loans that weren't on our books for the FDIC was one of the best deals we ever made.

We did not get the huge tax break afforded to NCNB when it acquired First Republic. No matter. In most other respects, the deals were similarly structured and equally generous, and the markets recognized it immediately. Our stock rose nearly fifteen percent on the day the deal was announced.

Before the MCorp deal, we were widely thought of as a very successful Midwestern bank. After it, we were anointed as the new darlings of Wall Street and American banking. You can still feel the surprise and excitement in how *The Wall Street Journal* reported the MCorp deal on June 29, 1989, almost as if a nag had won the Kentucky Derby:

> Banc One Corp., in a stunning entry into the Texas market, won the bidding war for MCorp's failed banks. …
>
> Banking experts hailed the deal as a major coup for Banc One, which in many ways patterned its bid after the highly successful entry of NCNB Corp. into Texas. …
>
> "Assuming we don't have a catastrophe in Texas, I don't see how they can go wrong," said Anthony Montelaro, who heads the Dallas office of Secura Group, a bank consulting company.
>
> The Ohio bank-holding company surprised many experts by surpassing a strong field of competitors. … Indeed, many had counted it out of the running entirely because it was bidding against several in-state organizations, who could presumably bring greater cost savings to the bargaining table.
>
> "It's hard to believe they put in the lowest-cost bid," said Frank Anderson, an analyst with Stephens Inc., Little Rock, Arkansas.

Texas was a real watershed event, primarily because the world didn't expect it. A hard-punching middleweight bank from the heartland had bested an international field of heavyweight contenders. It fit our style of saying less and delivering more. That way, when we did something, we got more credit. The MCorp deal reverberated in the marketplace and signaled that we had far greater aspirations than we'd previously let on.

MCorp would remain the core of our Texas holdings, but we had more room to grow. In 1990, we purchased the failed Bright Banc Savings from the Resolution Trust Corporation, a temporary government agency charged with liquidating the assets of failed financial institutions. The S&L's forty-eight branches were added to our sixty-three Texas branches at that time.

In 1992, we acquired the previously mentioned Team Bancshares of Dallas, a profitable company that was formed by Ron Steinhart's private investor group in 1988 to acquire failed and weak Texas banks, for $782 million in Banc One stock. The acquisition of Team Bank added another fifty-six branches to our 146 in Texas, though we had to close a few branches because of overlapping.

After this acquisition, Bank One Texas was a strong number two to the state's largest financial institution, NationsBank. Team Bank's Steinhart eventually replaced Hoaglin and Mitchell ran our franchise in Texas.

A few weeks after the MCorp transaction closed, Bill and I were in northern Michigan, where my family vacations during most summers. John G. was also there, and he sensed that Bill and I were feeling pretty good about ourselves as newly minted Texas bankers. We even threw in some good-natured chest bumps in his presence as we discussed the deal. Yes, we were riding high.

"Don't get too cocky; don't think you're the best," was father's reaction, with a half-smile and that piercing glance that could melt wax. He didn't want our egos to get too big. We knew he was right and in our hearts knew that our performance was just that—a little private celebration after several months of intense work and negotiations. We weren't planning on changing our style, but anytime you do a deal you feel pretty good. And this one was a great big deal.

People started to notice. After MCorp, I was regularly on the cover of every major financial newspaper and magazine in America. Banc One was praised as one of the best-run banks in the country with unmatched M&A

prowess. We were genuine media darlings. "The magnificent McCoys: Running America's best bank," was the cover story of the July 1991 *Institutional Investor* magazine, showcasing three generations of our family; "Banking's best acquirer" was the headline on a *Fortune* article that same month, celebrating our M&A skills and the power of the uncommon partnership; and *BusinessWeek* dubbed me "Banking's Golden Boy," based on the remarks of an institutional investor.

And under the headline "Master builder," *American Banker* proclaimed me "Banker of the Year" for 1992, with my portrait occupying the entire cover of the January 21, 1993 issue. At the age of 49, I had "just come off of a dream year," the article began, wrapping up some of the largest of our more than 100 acquisitions to date. "Acquisitions are a well-oiled line of business at Banc One, and Mr. McCoy has shown that he understands the difference between constructive assimilation and crude empire-building."

"John didn't take this company from seventy-first largest to seventh largest by being scared of his shadow," boasted our treasurer, George Meiling, who was interviewed for the article.

High praise, to be sure. You never hate it when someone is celebrating you, and all the industry accolades and media attention were most definitely gratifying. I was far from blind to all the attention we were getting. You bet I read those articles, and I still have many of them. But you try to remain humble and not get caught up in the hype. I never felt like I was the best, always believing that the best that I could be was still in front of me. My philosophy was to be like the captain of a ship, advocating a "steady as she goes" approach.

I wasn't the banking superhero I was being made out to be, but there's no question I was ambitious and wanted to build and run a great company that was recognized as such. If a CEO doesn't have that kind of drive and ambition, there's something wrong.

CHAPTER FOURTEEN

Westward Ho

I'm often asked how we did it. What made Banc One such a prolific and successful acquirer?

First and foremost, it was because we devoted tremendous resources to M&A. It was Bill's full-time job to identify, evaluate and negotiate deals. In boxing terms, he was my footwork and jab, and I was the uppercut.

"No bank had a person like me," Bill explained. "It was usually a function of the chief financial officer."

In the early days, when we were acquiring $100 million-asset banks in Ohio and Indiana, Bill would get the deals teed up and I would come in at the end and formalize everything with my counterpart. Sometimes I'd get involved earlier if that made the seller comfortable. But generally it was Bill laying the groundwork. We also had a team of analysts that scoured target-banks' financial statements so we could evaluate their business practices, loan portfolios, profitability and upside potential. That determined what we could afford to pay.

When you analyze a bank, you do what is called due diligence. It was key to every deal that we did. What we would do, big or small, was send people into every area of the bank and analyze how they ran each department. If we were looking at the commercial lending department, we would thoroughly review their loans to make sure their credit quality was sound, but we'd also look at other things such as loan pricing, fee structure and how they dealt with troubled loans. We would get reports back on what they did well and what they did poorly. We'd want our person who was reviewing that area to tell us, if they were running that department, what changes would they make and how much more money could they make. We would put together a book reviewing every aspect of the company and what the opportunities were to increase the profitability of that bank. On average we would only achieve fifty percent of what they said the potential was, but the fifty percent made our deals very successful. I didn't expect to get 100%, but what we did get usually worked out fine.

When people ask why we were better at M&A than our peers, it was because we had a road map of what we were going to do at every bank we acquired.

And of course, once banks were acquired, we had our Share and Compare system through which our affiliate banks were designated as mentors to newly acquired institutions, helping them to reach their goals and learn our ways.

Later, as we acquired ever larger banks and multi-bank holding companies, I got involved earlier and earlier in the negotiating process. And as the deals grew, we found ourselves working more with investment banks representing the sellers, and not the sellers themselves. Goldman Sachs was one that came to us many times on behalf of sellers. We rarely used investment banks as our intermediaries or representatives in the negotiating phase, however.

◄ *Previous page:* The 1993 acquisition of Phoenix-based Valley National Bank really extended our franchise and made Banc One the nation's eighth largest bank and No. 1 in fast-growing Arizona.

In 1991, we had the opportunity to acquire Arizona's largest bank, Valley National Corp., which was a wonderful franchise but had lost $149 million during a real estate downturn in 1989 and had come close to failing. Valley National Bank, which had about $11 billion in assets, was being pursued by Wells Fargo on an unfriendly basis. The folks at Valley National, led by CEO Richard Lehmann, knew they'd be out of work or marginalized if Wells or another West Coast bank succeeded, so they were interested in negotiating a better deal with us.

We took a look, and certainly liked Arizona's prospects for economic and population growth. That part was a no-brainer. What concerned us was the volume of bad real estate loans the company was working through. We were concerned that they had not fixed all their problems, so we told them we couldn't do the transaction.

Normally, you get one bite of the apple, and we assumed that by declining we wouldn't get a second chance. Valley would probably approach and strike a friendly deal with someone else. But eight months later, with Wells still lurking, Lehmann came back to us and said most of the problems had been fixed and that he'd still like to do the transaction. That spoke volumes about our reputation as an acquirer of choice. Because we were familiar with their loan portfolio, we could see the improvements they had made over the last eight months. We could have acquired them for a lot less had we done it the first time around, but we didn't want to risk our bottom line.

We sent forty of our people—commercial lenders primarily—to review Valley's financials and verify that problems with its real estate loans were declining. When we were satisfied that they were, we were able to agree on a price ($1.2 billion) without a bidding war between us and any other potential suitors. The Valley National deal closed in March 1993. Just like that, we were the nation's eighth largest bank and the No. 1 player in Arizona, leapfrogging ahead of western powerhouses Wells Fargo and BankAmerica.

Here's an excerpt from *The New York Times* when the deal was announced in April 1992, describing how cost savings and greater efficiency could be achieved:

Mr. McCoy, after 107 acquisitions and two decades of rising profits that have made Banc One one of Wall Street's favorite bank stocks, said he was confident that Valley would become more profitable under the Banc One umbrella. Within three to five years he predicted that Valley's profits would rise from 80 cents per $100 of assets to $1.25 ... about the average for Banc One's subsidiary banks.

Unlike many other bank mergers, Banc One does not envision closing branch offices or laying off employees. The only significant cut at Valley will be its computer-intensive data processing operation, which keeps track of customer transactions and balances and produces monthly account statements. Within two years Valley's data processing will be shifted to a processing center in Ohio for an annual savings of $20 million or more.

Although Valley has a reputation as a strong consumer bank—Banc One tried a few years ago to hire Richard D. Snewajs, head of retail banking at Valley—analysts expect there is enough room for improvement that Mr. McCoy's goals will be met.

"The people at Valley have been forced to spend so much time managing their bad credits that they ... lost some of their ability to focus on developing ... products and pricing strategies," said Moshe Ohrenbuch, an analyst at Sanford C. Bernstein & Company. "That is ... where Banc One can help with its Share and Compare policy."

Share and Compare refers to Banc One's practice of standardizing the products and accounting systems at its banking subsidiaries and encouraging its bankers to share the secrets of their successes and warn others of potential pitfalls.

By leaving each bank free to devise its own marketing strategies and prices, but requiring all banks to file monthly reports of their past results and forecasts, Banc One has found a way to leave local bankers with a sense of control, while the home office watches carefully enough to spot problems quickly.

CHAPTER FIFTEEN

Derivatives and Project One

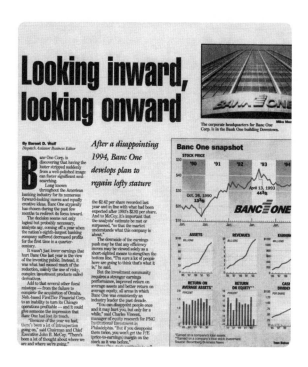

Nothing runs perfectly forever. Even a Lamborghini requires new spark plugs now and again. In 1993, our sports car of a company, having grown by leaps and bounds, hit its first real speed bump in the form of derivatives.

Derivatives are financial instruments that, if used properly, help to mitigate risk for large corporations, most notably banks and securities firms. They are contracts whose value is derived from the value of some underlying asset, which can be currencies, equities, commodities, even interest rates. Derivative instruments can be called swaps, forwards, futures, puts, calls and collars, among other names.

The idea was to manage interest-rate risk, to protect us if rates went way up or way down quickly. Derivatives were that hedge.

We began to rely on derivatives more heavily from 1989 on, after we acquired the failed MCorp banks in Texas. MCorp had lots of deposits but few good loans; and most of those paid variable rates. That left us exposed were rates to fall.

To offset this risk, we became a heavy user of interest-rate swaps, which allowed us to convert part of this variable-rate income stream to fixed rates. With rates falling, the strategy, combined with investments in fixed-rate securities, worked well. In 1992, for example, the investment positions contributed $91 million to income. But a year later, while the derivatives worked as intended, rates increased more and faster than we anticipated. Locked into the swaps, we lost money on those bets.

On November 21, 1994, we announced a $235 million after-tax restructuring charge, mostly due to a $170 million loss on the sale of $5.7 billion in securities to reverse our derivatives strategy. The sky was not exactly falling, mind you, as we would still earn about $1 billion that year. But the downturn ended our enviable streak of twenty-five straight years of steadily rising profits. Worse, the loss took the investment community by surprise. We had not previously disclosed our use of derivatives because there was no such requirement.

We were punished by Wall Street, which would probably prefer a giant asteroid crash into Earth than be hit with an earnings surprise. Within a few months, our stock had lost one-third of its value, severely limiting our ability to make the acquisitions that we thrived on.

"The market has signaled to us, stick to your core markets and don't try to guess interest rates," is how I put it to one interviewer.

People didn't understand derivatives then, and they still don't now. And when people don't understand something, they get nervous and sell your stock. We did our best to explain why we used derivatives, how our strategy

◄ *Previous page: The Columbus Dispatch,* more than any other newspaper, was there to tell the decades-long story of City National, FirstBanc Group, Banc One and the McCoys.

had gone against us, and what we were doing to fix it. We even hosted a two-day conference to explain everything to the analysts and media.

The stench from derivatives lingered for about a year. We weren't exactly tarred and feathered, but we went from wearing white hats to beige hats. Our stock had lost its premium to the market and our reputation was tarnished. We had a lot of fence mending with the investment community ahead, but we also turned our gaze inward.

The derivatives setback sparked a period of reassessment and soul searching, though in reality it was years in the making. In the decade since I became CEO, Banc One had grown from an Ohio-only bank with about $8 billion in assets into a sprawling financial institution of more than $100 billion in assets that was among the largest in the country.

We had taken advantage of interstate banking laws to enter new states and along the way benefitted from the economic misfortunes of others to make acquisitions. We had capitalized on our reputation as an "acquirer of choice" when other banks were fending off unwanted or hostile approaches, allowing important deals in Wisconsin and Arizona to come to us. We had grown like gangbusters.

But the old ways of local autonomy that had taken us so far were getting harder to manage as we grew. We had 88 bank presidents in thirteen states (more than twenty in Ohio alone) with much of the authority they enjoyed before being acquired by Banc One. (I used to joke that we had more bank presidents than Carter had little pills.) We had seventy-seven bank charters, twenty-two check-processing centers, eight money management divisions, six trust departments and four autonomous credit-card divisions, sometimes soliciting the same customers. Bank One branches around the country offered different products and services, and charged different fees, which was confusing to customers and difficult to administer. To take one example, we had 147 different checking account plans across our system. Just imagine if McDonald's had 147 variations of a Big Mac, or if a cup of coffee in Starbucks tasted slightly different in every store you visited.

Meanwhile, our decision making had become ossified. Historians say one reason the Ottoman Empire collapsed after six centuries was too much bureaucracy. While we hadn't quite reached empire levels of stagnation, there were clear warning signs. In the early 1990s we were planning a new cash management system for business customers, and it took three months to develop the proposal and fifteen more for all the affiliate banks to agree to the terms. Even a sultan would have been frustrated.

For these and other reasons, our costs had risen from fifty-five percent of revenue in 1990, which was best in the business, to sixty-five percent in 1994, among the worst.

Yes, we had succeeded spectacularly by allowing affiliates to run their own show as long as they met corporate-wide goals. But the multi-state Banc One of 1994 bore little resemblance to the plucky First Banc Group of the 1970s that combined small-town Ohio banks under a common banner. What had worked for my father, and for me in the early part of my career, had become a liability. Our operations were inefficient and bloated. There was no escaping it: The Uncommon Partnership had become an unwieldy partnership.

This hadn't suddenly dawned on me overnight. I recognized it as early as 1989, when we acquired Valley and Arizona became our thirteenth state. What took me so long to implement change? Tradition as much as anything. Remember what happened when Coca-Cola changed its 100-year-old formula and rebranded itself as "New Coke?" All hell broke loose and they retreated amid a customer revolt.

The Uncommon Partnership was woven into the fabric of our culture. It was our secret sauce. As we grew, it remained part of our identity and a major point of differentiation among the large banks. The Uncommon Partnership had served us well.

I experienced many sleepless nights pondering when and how to tackle this problem. Change was going to be costly, time-consuming and disruptive in the short-term. But with our M&A activities largely on pause following the derivatives losses of 1994, I decided the time was right to address these issues. It killed me to have to do it, but there was really no alternative. We needed a fix.

I wanted father to hear the plans from me. John G. was eighty-one at this point and very far removed from these types of decisions. Nonetheless, the Uncommon Partnership was his creation and a major part of his legacy. At a minimum I wanted him to be aware of it, and I certainly didn't want him to have to walk into a board meeting ill-prepared and hear him say, "You're going to do what?"

I called him up and said there was something we needed to discuss, and later that day I drove to his house in the Columbus bedroom community of New Albany.

"Dad, I think we need to change the structure of the company," is how I put it. With my stomach in a knot, I spent several minutes sketching out some of the reasons why I wanted to make changes. He listened, and to my relief did not seem surprised or upset.

When I was done, he said, "Carry on."

My conversations with my father were always pretty brief, so this was hardly unusual. It felt good to get it out in the open.

Years later, he told a magazine interviewer that the decision was sound. "I think (John B.) had concerns over whether I would agree with him or not," father said. "I had to agree. He was on the right track."

We called the reorganization plan Project One, which was put together over several months by Don McWhorter, president of the holding company, in consultation with me and senior leaders of the company. It was a thoughtful, deliberative process, which was a relief to our managers even though they knew there would be winners and losers. People were nervous, and rightly so.

Project One was unveiled in a speech given by me in February 1994 and viewed live by nearly 1,500 employees in a closed-circuit broadcast. It called for the elimination of the state and regional structures, replacing them with five line-of-business organizational structures that were more typical of a large multistate company. The lines of business were retail banking, commercial banking, credit card, investment products and specialty lending.

Purchasing, operations, product design and marketing would all be run out of Columbus. Bank presidents would become market managers for a sales district. While they would still be measured by the overall profitability of their regions, more of their compensation would be based on sales volume rather than cost cutting. We wanted to centralize most consumer lending activities, retaining local authority for business loans only.

We hoped to achieve $500 million annually in savings by 1999 through a combination of greater efficiency and job cuts of around 5,000. It was a SlimFast diet and I was passing out cups and asking everyone to drink up. It was probably the toughest decision I ever had to make at the bank.

Wall Street generally loves a good austerity plan as a way to boost profitability, especially after a company has undergone a multiyear growth spree as we had. The reason? Effective pruning can produce new shoots and more vigor. But there was an underlying wariness in our case as it pertained to Project One.

"Moving away from the Uncommon Partnership has its risks," a Morgan Stanley banking analyst told *The New York Times*. The main concern was whether centralization would make Banc One indistinguishable from a dozen other large banks. Wouldn't it be difficult to justify a significantly higher stock price than our competitors, the article asked, and could we continue to "woo bank executives into selling their companies" if they lost their autonomy?

These were fair questions and precisely why we had resisted change for so long.

Internally, I was very much aware of how the transition to a centralized management structure would be difficult for our people to adapt to. We had lots of managers who were very good at what they did in Akron, Ohio, or Madison, Wisconsin, but weren't necessarily the best in the business to run a much bigger enterprise after consolidation. This tested me as a CEO. I had to balance my loyalty to my people with what I believed was best for the corporation.

Our 1,500 retail branches were going to be the biggest piece of the organizational puzzle and a priority. While we had one of the largest branch networks in the country, no one person at Banc One ran more than 200 branches, because of our decentralized structure. I wasn't convinced we had someone internally who could run the whole thing. It would have been a very big step up. So we hired a headhunter to help me find someone capable of leading this far-flung national business.

We spoke with executives from Bank of America and other large competitors who were doing similar things, but I wasn't sold on any of them. Banc One was more sales oriented, innovative and entrepreneurial than the typical large bank. I suggested that we look outside of financial services to find someone who knew how to run large systems and keep them fresh. Any systems.

We ended up hiring Ken Stevens, who was president and chief operating officer of Taco Bell. Ken was very successful at managing a fast-growing and innovative enterprise for PepsiCo, so I felt there was no reason why he couldn't wrap his mind around bank branches. After all, both businesses had busy drive-up windows and customers who wanted to get in and out and be greeted with a smile. Both had competition on every corner and needed to stand out in a crowd. I told him I didn't care if he couldn't make a loan, because I was pretty sure that he didn't know how to cook a taco either.

There's always a personal component to managing change, and good managers are sensitive to it. I refused to turn my back on those Banc One managers who had done acceptable work for many years but weren't going to make it to the next level as we nationalized our business. If I couldn't promote somebody, I'd be willing to work with him or her. If they weren't the best, I'd sit down and have a conversation that would go something like this: "You've done a very capable job of running a $5 billion line of business, but I'm not convinced you can run a $20 billion line of business, and here's why." We'd go over all the specifics.

I'd tell my manager or salesperson that if I could find someone who I felt was fifty percent better for the new role, I was going to bring that new person in. "If that happens, I'd like you to stay for a year," I'd say. Often times, in that year, the person would learn so much that it made him or her a better employee. If after a year, he or she didn't feel that way, I'd try to help that person find another job. But as it turns out, most people chose to stay.

Those are difficult decisions to make and tough conversations to have. But employees appreciate and respect that kind of honesty from a boss. I can't tell you how many people I helped to get new jobs with competitors, something I'm very proud of.

Project One would take several years to implement. Not every goal was met or every efficiency achieved. But we made great strides in setting standards across the company and offering unified products and services to our customers regardless of what market they were in. We didn't defeat bureaucracy, but we tamed it.

I'll admit to this: It was a lot more fun growing the company from 1983 to 1995 than it was reformulating the company for the next five years. We made big changes and lost some of the flavor of the Uncommon Partnership as we centralized, but I'm still convinced that the changes were necessary and made Banc One a stronger company.

With our reorganization underway and our stock back on the rise, we felt comfortable in resuming our M&A activities around the 1995 timeframe. We weren't aggressively beating the bushes, yet one of our first opportunities came to us. It wasn't the biggest deal we'd ever consider, but it was the most gratifying for my father, who was still on our board.

You may recall that in the 1950s, both my father and his younger brother Chuck helped my grandfather, John H. McCoy, run scrappy little City National in Columbus. City National was a weak No. 3 in town in those days, and the brothers were behind a number of innovations, including the first bank branch in the country designed from the ground up with multiple drive-thru banking windows. They also were the ones who removed the bars from the teller windows and made the inside of a bank less like a jail and more like a place your neighbors would want to visit.

When grandfather died in 1958, it was John G. who was hired by the board to run City National. Yearning to make a name for himself, Uncle Chuck left City National and Columbus a year later to join Baton Rouge-based Louisiana National Bank, later to become Premier Bancorp. Within two years of his arrival Chuck McCoy was promoted to president. Under his leadership the bank was the first in the state to install an ATM and one of the first in the nation to issue debit cards, proving that you could take the McCoy out of City National but you couldn't take the City National out of the McCoy.

By every measure Uncle Chuck was a successful bank president, but one achievement really stands out: Under his internal training program, thirty-four junior executives went on to become bank presidents.

By 1995, Uncle Chuck was well into retirement and Lee Griffin was running Premier. As with Texas, Louisiana's fortunes were very much tied to energy. Here's how *American Banker* described what was happening:

> Ravaged by a plunge in energy prices in the 1980s, the state emerged as a sobering case study on the dangers of being overly reliant on one industry, in this case oil and gas. Local economies languished, businesses floundered and the state's four largest banks—once-stellar performers—found themselves mired in a pool of bad loans like pelicans trapped in an oil spill. One-third of the state's financial institutions perished from 1982 to 1992.

Despite a strong franchise in key Louisiana markets, Premier became unprofitable in 1986 when oil prices dropped forty-seven percent in the year's first quarter alone. Losses continued and reached $106 million in 1989. The $5.5 billion asset bank with 150 branches returned to profitability in 1990, but it needed a capital infusion amid continuing bad loans, or it was going to fail.

In early 1991, I got a call from Griffin. "John, I'd like to come and talk to you," he began. "We're still in trouble. I think we've got a solution to our problem, but we may need your help. And I have to ask you not to tell your uncle and not to tell your father that I'm talking to you."

This was curious. "Lee, I have no reason to talk to Chuck, but if we start negotiating I'm going to have to tell the board and I'll have to tell my father. We can have a conversation, because I have a lot of conversations with a lot of bankers, and I don't have to tell anybody about it, and what I will promise you is when I have to tell my father I will tell you first, so if you want to cut off the transaction you can cut off the transaction, and that's fine." He was satisfied and wanted to proceed.

Bill Boardman and I were in Texas looking for add-on acquisitions for MCorp, and we arranged for Lee and his team to come visit us in our hotel suite at 7:30 a.m. the next morning. Bill wanted to get a head start and was reviewing some Premier documents. He had a keen eye and didn't like what he was seeing.

"John, I know we've got this meeting with those guys tomorrow, and I know it's your uncle and everything, but I hope you're not gonna do this deal just because of that," he began. "Because this would be the worst deal that I've ever seen. I'm scared to death you're going to make a terrible deal."

Whoa. That was strong stuff from the usually understated Bill.

"Now Bill," I reassured him. "You and I, before every negotiation, we always sit down and we agree on what the number is. We never change the number in the meeting unless we both step out and agree to change the number. I agree with you about Premier, but I want to have this meeting and at about eight o'clock I'm going to tell them that we can't do the deal."

Bill was relieved. "Oh, I'm so glad for that."

The next day we started the meeting at 7:30. Griffin's people began by reviewing a chamber of commerce report that said, predictably, that things were going to be better in Louisiana, you just wait and see. I'm thinking, ugh, this is going nowhere.

Then Griffin played a stronger card. "Let us show you what we've done," he began. "We've mapped every loan for the last three years, and we've rated every loan for the last three years, and we can show you we're right on track. The charge-offs are going to be exactly where we said they'd be three years ago."

This was news to us. We were very familiar with Premier and had great respect for the franchise, but we anticipated the overall economic conditions in the state were going to continue to be a drag on them. Now it looked like the situation had stabilized and they were working through their bad loans. And if the state's economy had turned a corner, so much the better.

Suddenly I felt someone kicking my leg under the table. It was Bill. "Lee, can I borrow John for just one second, I thought of something and we'll be right back in."

We stepped out of the room. "I think this stuff is really good, maybe a potential deal for us," a wide-eyed Bill said.

We ended up putting together a very creative deal, and Banc One agreed to acquire Premier for just over $700 million in stock. When we had finished, I said, "Lee, you've got to tell Chuck whatever you need to tell him, because I'm going to tell John G."

Father was very pleased to be adding his brother's former bank to the fold. Not in a boastful or competitive way, but as a genuine family reunion of sorts. He would never have wanted to force such a union if it wasn't in the best interest of both banks, and it was.

John G. got to join us in Louisiana when we closed the deal, and Uncle Chuck was present as well. They sure had fun together. Chuck had set out on his own because City National wasn't big enough for both of them, but they always remained great brothers and great friends. The transaction brought things full circle. It was gratifying to see and I was happy to be part of it.

"I would have sold to anybody who was interested," Chuck said at one point, needling his brother a little bit. "But I think you guys are the right people to sell to." We could all drink to that.

CHAPTER SIXTEEN

Let's Not Make a Deal

Though we began as a pure Midwestern bank with a consumer focus, by the mid-'90s we were much more than that, having made huge bets on new geographies and new lines of business including selling stocks and bonds to our customers. In truth we were open to opportunities anywhere in the country.

For example, we considered buying the Bank of New England, kicked the tires of Florida-based Barnett Banks and considered Washington-based Puget Sound Bancorp. These were unique markets with entrenched players and challenges all their own. We seriously explored a "merger of equals" with Pittsburgh's PNC Bank Corp., a bank of similar size and scope that we competed with in Ohio, Indiana, Michigan and elsewhere. PNC had a corporate culture similar to ours and boasted a commanding presence in Pennsylvania, western

New York and other markets where we were lacking. The combination would have solidified our position in the Midwest while serving as a springboard to additional growth throughout the New England and mid-Atlantic regions.

CEO Tom O'Brien was a good friend and occasional golfing partner of mine. We were both in Pebble Beach, California, for a banking conference, and Tom asked me if we could speak privately about something that was on his mind. "I think we ought to have a conversation," he said in the typically vague way that CEOs approached these matters.

Later on in his hotel room (it was plenty big and no one had to sit on the bed), he sketched out his plans for a combination. Banc One would technically be the acquiring entity, as we were larger and more profitable, and I would be CEO. He would be chairman. So far, so good.

There was a catch. The headquarters would have to be in Pittsburgh. Would we be willing to pull up stakes and move our people from Columbus to Pittsburgh, he asked. I told him I would think about it.

Any headquarters move is time-consuming, gut-wrenching and expensive. Would the ends justify the means? Bill Boardman and I spent many hours discussing the pros and cons of the deal. There were many more pros—tremendous cost savings from combining two similar companies, minimal geographic overlap and the chance to create a truly national franchise, to name a few. But under what circumstances would we consider moving our headquarters for a deal? This was something we had not previously contemplated in much depth.

We came to the conclusion that Pittsburgh—which is a great city and home to many corporations—wasn't enough of an upgrade from Columbus to justify the disruption and expense of moving the headquarters. Pittsburgh was not as centrally located for our company as Columbus, and held no particular advantage for recruitment of talent or for its business climate. For us,

◄ *Previous page:* Deals we considered but never proceeded with included partnerships with Pittsburgh-based PNC and San Francisco's Wells Fargo. Many factors, including culture and geography, are weighed by dealmakers.

moving to Pittsburgh was a lateral move at best, so we declined. As a result, the conversations fizzled.

The PNC offer did get us thinking about the possibility of moving the headquarters, and under what circumstances it could make sense. Such a move would need to be advantageous to the business in two ways: one, if it facilitated a meaningful acquisition, and two, if the location was clearly superior in a measurable way.

Some moves don't accomplish anything. Consider SBC Communications, the telephone company, which was based in St. Louis until it moved its corporate headquarters to San Antonio, Texas, in 1993. (The CEO who made the decision was a Texan who had a ranch near San Antonio, if you must know.) From a pure business standpoint, this was no upgrade. St. Louis was a bigger city, arguably more cosmopolitan and with easier access to most of the country for business travelers.

Fifteen years later, SBC acquired AT&T, adopted that name and once again moved its headquarters—this time to Dallas. Now you or I might think that San Antonio is a better place to live or work for any number of personal reasons. But for an international corporation like AT&T, Dallas is a far superior location, primarily because it's easier to recruit the very best talent. (In the interest of full disclosure, I was on the board of AT&T when the headquarters moved from San Antonio to Dallas, and I was in favor of it. You couldn't get to San Antonio.)

I had a similar problem at Banc One when it came to convincing leading lights in the banking business to leave New York, San Francisco or Chicago to move to Columbus. To many of them, Ohio's capital city was a backwater. Now, the funny thing was, once I got these guys to leave New York for Columbus, and later asked them to move to Texas or Arizona for a new assignment, most would say, "I'm not leaving Columbus, this is the best place I've ever been."

In the course of the PNC talks we concluded that Chicago would be the one place where it would make sense to relocate for the right deal. We didn't have a deal in mind at that time, although that eventually came to pass, and moving the headquarters was part and parcel of the 1998 deal with First Chicago-NBD. Our thinking was that as much as we loved Columbus, Chicago was a transportation hub, a financial center and of course the largest city in the Midwest. Bottom line: it was the best place for attracting talent and the most logical place for the largest bank in the Midwest to be located.

We also had another intriguing opportunity on the M&A front, a real "what if" to ponder. I was in Monterey, California, playing in a golf tournament, when I got a call from Paul Hazen, the CEO of San Francisco-based Wells Fargo and a good friend of mine then and now.

"I need to talk to you this afternoon," Paul said. "Can you meet me at the airport terminal?" He was referring to the private terminal in Monterey, which is about 125 miles south of San Francisco. He would fly there to meet with me.

It must have been important for him to call me so urgently on short notice, so I agreed. "Absolutely," I said.

I was dying of curiosity by the time we met at the airport, but of course I had an inkling that something was up. Nothing happens if you don't talk and listen, so I was all ears.

Paul told me that Minneapolis-based US Bancorp was pursuing him, and was prepared to make an unfriendly bid if he didn't respond. Paul was concerned that he had no way to counter the bid, because US Bancorp could afford to pay. They were going to come in, push him out, and run the business the way they wanted to. Paul confided that he was also speaking with Ed Crutchfield, CEO of Charlotte-based First Union, which later became Wachovia.

While they were discussing a possible combination, one or both of them came up with the idea of including Banc One in a three-way partnership. Would I be interested in a three-way deal, he wanted to know.

I tried to be polite, though I'm sure the skepticism was written all over my face. "You know," I began, "I can't say that I've seen any three-way deals." In fact I'd never heard of one.

Paul wasn't deterred. He told me this would be a grand deal that I had to consider.

"OK," I said. "Get Crutchfield out here on Sunday, and I'll get Boardman to come out and we'll go through it."

Bill flew out and we had the meeting. "How would you guys make decisions?" I inquired of my counterparts, to which Crutchfield replied: "We'll work together."

That was awfully murky. "I don't understand how we'll work together," I remarked. "Who's going to be CEO?"

"You'll be CEO," Hazen said. "Everybody hates us but they think you're God, so you be the CEO."

That came as a surprise. "Well, that's an interesting idea," I acknowledged. "Do you have a name? I'm not locked into Banc One."

Hazen was ready: "The name will be Wells Fargo."

OK, I thought, things were getting interesting. It was obvious that these guys had thought things through. What else has been decided, I wondered.

"How do we decide where to have the headquarters?" I asked. "Since Paul's in San Francisco and you're in Charlotte," I said, looking at Crutchfield, "maybe we could have it in Dallas," which was a neutral spot and a good locale, since Banc One was now the second-largest bank in Texas.

Crutchfield smiled and leaned forward. "You know," he began. "We lost the Civil War, and we're not going to lose the headquarters. It's going to be in Charlotte." Now that was some reasoning! I almost fell over.

We went back and forth for another hour and eventually concluded there would be no transaction. The thought of a combination was fascinating to be sure, but we all knew deep down that it wasn't workable. We made for strange bedfellows. Those guys would have been a lot to handle for any CEO, and there wouldn't have been enough aspirin in the world to overcome the headaches that would have resulted. The whole idea was just so over the top.

(In case you're wondering what became of US Bancorp's pursuit of Wells Fargo, it never came to pass. Hazen was able to strike a deal with a cross-town rival of US Bancorp's, Norwest Corp., to combine on a "merger of equals" basis and keep the Wells Fargo name and San Francisco headquarters. US Bancorp would have likely paid more, but by negotiating with Norwest, Wells Fargo management was able to preserve the name, headquarters and employment, which would not have been the case if US Bancorp did a hostile deal.)

Another opportunity was my initiative. Dean Witter Reynolds was one of the premier retail brokerage businesses in the country, right up there with Merrill Lynch, way before the internet altered the landscape and gave rise to the discount and online brokers that dominate the retail business today. Dean Witter had been part of Sears (after a probably misguided 1981 takeover), but by the mid-'90s it had been spun off and was an independent company again.

When it became legal for us to own a brokerage firm, I thought that buying a large brokerage business made a lot of sense. I knew I was going to bump into Dean Witter's CEO Phil Purcell on an upcoming weekend. When I did, I said, "Phil, I've got an idea for you. I think it would be interesting if we put our two companies together. In fact, I've got a four page write-up as to why it's smart." Bill had helped me to put together the business-case memo.

A week passed and I heard nothing from Purcell. Bill was going absolutely crazy. Why hadn't we heard?

The following week I was again scheduled to be at a meeting where I would see Purcell. "Phil, what did you think of my write-up?" I inquired when I saw him.

"It's still in my briefcase. I never read it," he replied. "I never thought that I'd ever want to merge with a bank." That stung a little.

Now I believe that he had read the write-up and simply wasn't interested. I wasn't wild about the way he handled it, but everyone's different. A year later Dean Witter bought Morgan Stanley to create the country's largest securities firm, so at least I could understand why he had been so dismissive of me. He had had a plan of his own, so good for him.

CHAPTER SEVENTEEN

One That Got Away

With our reorganization underway and our stock on the rise, we felt comfortable in resuming our M&A activities starting around 1995. The year had certainly started off with a bang for some of our peers, and we were eager to rejoin the party after our self-imposed M&A moratorium.

In February, in a merger of two big Eastern banks, Fleet Financial agreed to acquire Shawmut National for $3.7 billion. In June, Charlotte-based First Union announced what was then the largest bank merger ever, agreeing to pay $5.4 billion for First Fidelity Bancorp of Newark, N.J. That combination would create an East Coast giant stretching from Connecticut to Florida.

While we admired these transactions greatly, we understood that they made more sense for the buyers than they would have made for us. That's because these were in-market deals for the buyers, so they would have had a lot more cost savings to achieve than we could have. Any pain we felt at not getting those deals was tempered by the reality that there were better transactions for us closer to home.

Three weeks after the First Union-First Fidelity deal, a third deal went down—this time in our own back yard—that threw us for a loop.

Illinois and Michigan were two states in which we had had the least success to this point. Chicago-based First Chicago Corp. was the top dog in Illinois, while Detroit's NBD Bancorp (formerly National Bank of Detroit) was the leading bank in Michigan. In the mid-1990s, we remained an insignificant player in both markets.

There was no particular reason for this; it was more a matter of timing and what had been available. We had taken advantage of great opportunities in Indiana, Kentucky, Wisconsin and even Texas and Arizona without finding similar openings in Illinois and Michigan. Both were absolutely in our plans and we always thought we'd succeed there. We were patient and willing to bide our time.

First Chicago was an old-line commercial bank steeped in local history. It had been around for a long time, having extended loans to help rebuild Chicago after the Great Fire of 1871. While First Chicago had a noteworthy credit card business, retail banking was something of an afterthought. Remember that Illinois banking laws had limited financial institutions to a single branch in one county, so it only made sense that a large bank in a metro area like Chicago would cater to corporations and have less experience with branch banking.

NBD had a similar commercial focus in greater Detroit. It did a considerable amount of lending to automakers and other capital-intensive businesses. But because Michigan banking laws were less restrictive than those in Illinois, NBD had developed a better retail branch network in Michigan and Indiana.

◄ *Previous page:* I was disappointed that we didn't get a chance to bid on NBD, Michigan's largest bank, which was acquired by First Chicago to form Chicago-based First Chicago NBD. But we would meet again.

Either one would have been a great pickup for Banc One.

On July 13, 1995 (in the midst of the O.J. Simpson trial, no less), I awoke to the news that First Chicago and NBD had agreed to merge. The $5.3-billion deal would create the nation's seventh-largest bank-holding company and become the dominant bank in Illinois, Michigan and Indiana, with assets of $120 billion.

Boy, was I steamed. From my perspective this was humiliating on two fronts. For starters, I was very familiar and even friendly with both of the CEOs who had put together the deal. Secondly, I learned about the merger in the newspaper (no internet news back then). The fact that neither chose to come to me with an offer or at least to discuss their situation felt like an affront. And there's nothing more irritating than reading about a deal that you could have done over your morning coffee. Missing out on any deal hurts, and this one was downright excruciating.

We didn't miss on many such opportunities, which made this major loss all the more surprising and painful. I would estimate that 95 percent of the time we would have a bite of the apple in all potential deals in our markets. What I mean by that is we would have either been approached to do a deal or known about deals in progress—in other words, in a position to participate if we wanted. Of course we frequently walked away, but we almost always had our chances.

There was open speculation for years that First Chicago needed a merger partner because the bank's growth prospects and earnings were less than spectacular, leaving it vulnerable to a hostile bid. I'd had friendly conversations with both of the CEOs in the course of the year, and they both knew that Banc One was a willing and able merger partner. Yet this corporate marriage was consummated without as much as a furtive glance my way.

Why so hush-hush? Outwardly, it was a logical combination of two neighboring commercial banks. That's often called a cultural fit. Combining McDonald's and Burger King would be a cultural fit, but combining McDonald's with an upscale steakhouse would not be.

But ultimately, it was what I call social issues for the executives themselves that brought these two companies together. Both CEOs—Dick Thomas of First Chicago and Charles "Chick" Fisher from NBD—were of retirement age and ready to step aside, allowing Verne Istock, the number two guy at NBD, to become chairman and CEO of the combined companies. The arrangement was ideal for the executives involved and an easy sell for investors and board members.

A deal with Banc One would not have paved the way for Istock's "monkey move up" to CEO. That's why neither bank wanted to talk to us, even though we almost certainly would have paid more for either company. And that only added to our frustration over this lost opportunity.

What was behind the flurry of big deals of 1995? One important factor was that federal legislation had passed the previous year allowing full-scale interstate banking, making it easier for banks to rapidly gain market share by purchasing rivals in other states. This trumped the state barriers that had kept us bottled up in Ohio for so long.

Secondly, banks were "bulking up" in anticipation of Congress repealing the Glass-Steagall Act, the Depression-era federal law separating commercial banking from securities underwriting. We all expected the repeal of Glass-Steagall to unleash a frenzy of mergers between banks, brokerage firms and insurance companies. By undertaking more regional mergers ahead of the changes, the big players were making defensive plays to gain scale so they would stand a better chance of being the predator and not the prey should Glass-Steagall fall. (Some provisions were repealed in 1999.)

One banking analyst told *The Los Angeles Times* that in his opinion First Chicago's deal with NBD was "a defensive consolidation that turned them into the largest fish in the Midwestern pond," and safe for the time being from hostile bids. But like any good fisherman, a skilled dealmaker bides his time.

PART THREE
Big Game Hunting

CHAPTER EIGHTEEN

First USA

After the First Chicago-NBD wakeup call, Bill and I redoubled our efforts to get back in the game. It took some doing, and when we finally did make our next major move, we made quite a splash.

As previously mentioned, by the mid-1990s Banc One had four separate credit-card divisions serving different parts of the company. Columbus was home to our original card business dating back to the City National days, but there were similar operations we had inherited through acquisitions in Indiana, Arizona and Wisconsin. Each group was certain it was better than the others.

As independent fiefdoms, they were often in competition. Indiana would solicit Ohio customers and vice versa. In truth, even though we made a lot of money from credit cards, we were not best in class. I wondered whether our next big move should be in credit cards, a highly profitable business that we knew well.

Banks had traditionally been the issuers of credit cards, and of course Banc One was a pioneer from way back in the 1960s when father got that first BankAmericard franchise for Ohio. By now our credit card operations were inefficient and lacked focus. Project One had identified this as a problem, but we had not settled on a solution.

Meanwhile, a new crop of "pure play" credit card companies that did only one thing were becoming leaders in the business. They were MBNA, Capital One and First USA. These pure plays had become the real innovators in the space. We were falling behind in this important area, and we could not afford to, because in those days credit cards accounted for about one-third of our profits.

I hired an outside consulting firm to come look at our card business. After a few months of studying us, the lead guy came to see me and said, "John, we're going to propose next week that you get out of the credit-card business."

Not what I wanted to hear. To me, that was like telling McDonald's to stop making french fries because a few batches were too salty. Sure, I knew we didn't have the sophistication or critical mass to compete with the three big credit card companies. But to get out of such an important line of business was a non-starter.

"That's impossible," I replied. "We're a retail bank, and credit cards are retail. We can't do that."

"Alright, here's an idea," he said. (Consultants are nothing if not flexible.) "What if I come back and say that you've got to *buy* a credit card company to give you the critical mass you need to compete?"

"Perfect," I said.

◄ *Previous page:* Building a premier credit card business was the motivation behind our 1997 acquisition of First USA, our largest deal to date. It created a top-three card issuer with 32 million customers.

Now we were getting somewhere. Call me manipulative if you must, because I was absolutely steering the consultant toward my position so I could use his findings to convince the board and senior people that we should buy a leading card company and fold our businesses into it.

You might be wondering why the CEO would need a consultant to make this case for him. The short answer is that each of our credit card divisions had entrenched management and employees who thought they were the best and should be running the whole thing. Some of our board members had come from those banks with credit card operations, and they would be protective of their home states. There would be winners and losers in a unified card business, and that uncertainty always breeds resistance.

There are times, and I recognized this as one of them, when change is a lot easier to implement if a third party identifies the course to follow. Kind of like when my father asked the board to recommend to him the next leader of retail lending—hoping (and even expecting) that they would pick me—rather than for him to simply hire his son.

Sure, I thought it made sense to put everything together, but it would have more validity in the eyes of employees, management and the board if an outsider said so, too. After the consultant issued his report, everybody in the bank understood that we needed to put our card businesses together, and everybody said, "Great idea. Let's buy a credit card company."

Just as we always did with banks we wanted to buy, Bill and I began to approach the big credit card companies for preliminary discussions. We started right in our back yard—with MBNA, the nation's premier card issuer.

Al Lerner, the billionaire founder and owner of MBNA, was happy to meet with us and invited us to his Cleveland office. Bill and I donned the aw-shucks personas of folks seeking wisdom from an old master.

"Al, we're looking at what we should do with our credit card business, and we're wondering if it makes sense to put our businesses under one roof," I began. Of course I actually wanted to buy his business, but I didn't go there. In my heart of hearts, I was hoping Lerner would see tremendous value in a combination with us. But Lerner wasn't looking to sell MBNA. He was doing just fine and didn't need our financial backing.

He was abrupt and fairly dismissive. "Have you talked to First USA?" he interjected. "You should try to buy them." With one deft pin prick, my trial balloon was returning to earth.

We got the message, which was a bit humbling. Lerner must not have been taking us too seriously. Did he really want us to buy one of his chief rivals? Wouldn't that be a threat to him? He must not have thought so.

We thanked him for his time and were on our way. We had not spoken with First USA, but they were next on our list.

Dallas-based First USA was the nation's third-largest card issuer with 16 million customers and $22.4 billion in outstanding loans, about twice the size of our card business at the time. It was created in the 1980s as a spin-off from MCorp, which as you recall, we acquired as a failed Texas bank from the FDIC in 1990. After getting the boot at MBNA, we contacted First USA's chairman, John Tolleson, who said he was willing to meet with us the week after Christmas 1996. The location would be his vacation home in Vail, Colorado.

We tried to learn as much about these guys as we could ahead of the meeting. For starters, they were masters of direct mail. While we also tried to do direct mail, these guys were outstanding. They knew that if you had *Visa* on the back of the envelope they sent you, they got a response one-tenth of a percent higher than if the back of the solicitation said *MasterCard*. It was a level of sophistication that we simply didn't have.

First USA further distinguished itself by marketing to niche groups through co-branded "affinity cards" targeting club members, team fans or purchasers of a certain product or service. I remember they had an Ohio State University-First USA affinity card even though the OSU campus was just a few miles from our corporate headquarters. How did we miss that one? They had about 400 similar affinity cards while we had done three. Just a more impressive operation all the way around.

With an annual growth rate of about twenty-five percent, First USA was a real gem. And unlike the billionaire Al Lerner, Tolleson (who was forty-nine at the time) was indeed interested in doing a deal with a large bank such as ours. Why? First USA was a very successful business but it was always on the lookout for financial backing to support its lending. Let me explain.

At the bank, if I loaned you $100, where did I get this money? Primarily from deposits—certificates of deposit, savings and checking accounts. On the other hand, First USA and other pure-play card issuers had no deposits and got their money from commercial paper or other lenders, generally at a higher cost than I had to pay my depositors.

In addition to the higher cost of funds, there was the question of availability. Tolleson was concerned that if there were a credit crunch they wouldn't be able to fund their lending. If the securitization markets weakened, funding could dry up, while we would still have our deposits. They were always looking over their shoulder, wondering where their next billion dollars in funding would come from. This was the Achilles heel of an otherwise brilliant business.

For example, the financial crisis and Great Recession of 2007-09 would have murdered them when access to capital dried up. First USA wasn't worried about building their credit-card business, they were worried about funding it. That was the impetus for doing a deal with us or someone similar.

By joining us, they thought they could make more money with a reliable source of funding and a lower cost of funds. In addition, they thought they could make us better at credit cards, which would make Banc One more profitable. So there was plenty of upside for everyone.

Bill and I flew to Vail for the first meeting with Tolleson and Dick Vague, the company's chief operating officer and creative genius, so to speak. It was great because no one would know why were in Vail—First USA was based in Dallas and the bulk of its operations were in Delaware. You never wanted word to leak out that you were meeting about a potential acquisition, and this setting was off the beaten path.

Our objective in that or any first conversation was always to have a second conversation, because if you don't have a second conversation you haven't gotten anyplace. The first meeting is generally warm and fuzzy, with both sides saying why they are so great and why a combination will be great for everyone. Both sides have to leave the first meeting wanting another date and with the feeling that this marriage could work.

In my experience, most of the good negotiators are good conversationalists. I get along with most people and love to tell a good story. It's all part of the mating dance, as I liked to call these negotiations.

We had a great story to tell and had a lengthy track record. It wasn't just our word, it was our deeds. There were dozens of deals that we had done, so Tolleson or anyone else could go and check with the people who had sold to us and be reassured that John McCoy will do what he says he's going to do.

We were perceived as honest, straight shooters, in a business where a lot of people cut corners. Nobody ever questioned us about that, and that was huge.

One of the things sellers fear is that all of their people will lose their jobs. That was clearly not going to be the case with First USA because of their superior talent. If anything, some of our credit card people might be at risk of losing their jobs after this transaction, something I would have to grapple with.

Because Tolleson was already thinking about a merger of some sort when we approached him, things were moving along quite fast. At that first meeting we not only agreed that the transaction could have merit, but he told us what he thought his company was worth. "We want you to pay us $100 a share," he said, which was a considerable premium over where First USA stock was trading. That would be valuing First USA in the vicinity of $8 billion. Expressing a value so early on was a bit unusual, but not necessarily a bad sign.

"Well, maybe," I replied. "But let's see some numbers first. We have to see why it's worth a hundred."

Bill Boardman was a great negotiator, and a perfect foil to me. When price was being ironed out, Bill often played the good cop to my bad cop. (We could switch roles if need be.)

Most of the time he would frame up deals without me. Armed with his extensive knowledge of a target, he would have a value in mind. Alone with the seller, he might say, "Let's not take this to McCoy just yet, let's get this figured out here." Then when I joined the group at the next meeting, he could turn to me with a wary expression, as if I were a listing Hindenburg ready to explode, and say, "I told them you're not going to like this." Sometimes I'd wince or close my eyes after he relayed the asking price.

Of course this was theatrics. While we never knew the exact outcome of negotiations in advance, we had a game plan. Before any such meeting, Bill and I would agree on the amount we would pay. And then we would go into the meeting and negotiate to that number. Neither one of us would ever commit, in a meeting, to a higher number than we had determined in advance. Our competitors didn't know about that, but that's how we did it. If the target demanded a higher number, then Bill and I would reconsider in private. Fiscal discipline served us well and was a key to our success.

After the first meeting in Vail we agreed we would get a small team and meet up with their people in Dallas. We had that meeting a week or so later and then another one a week after that. There was genuine interest on both sides, but negotiating with the First USA folks was different. This wasn't a bank and they did a number of things that we didn't know very well or understand in great detail.

If I bought a bank and the top five people died in an airplane crash (thankfully this never happened), I could put my own people in there the next day. We would lose relationships, but I could run the business. But if the top five guys from First USA disappeared overnight, especially in the first two years after an acquisition, I was concerned that we couldn't run the business.

Tolleson was based in Dallas and was a very polished, big-picture guy. He had spent twenty-five years with the company, initially when it was the credit-card subsidiary of MCorp and after it was sold to Lomas Financial in 1986. Tolleson led a management buyout of the business from Lomas, and then took First USA public in 1992.

Vague worked in Delaware and was the idea guy who oversaw day-to-day operations. Dick Vague had 100 ideas a day, and Tolleson was very adept at weeding out the ninety-nine bad ones. They worked extremely well together.

Tolleson wanted to step away after a sale, but we wanted to keep them both. In the end, we agreed to let Tolleson take a seat on the Banc One board and relinquish his First USA duties. In this way we believed we could satisfy his desires and protect our interests as well.

Bill and our negotiating team held several more meetings with Vague and Tolleson in Vail and in Dallas, avoiding Wilmington because that's where all the senior staff was located and the chance of word leaking out would be higher. These were very technical meetings, focusing on a detailed review of the business, referred to as due diligence, and final negotiations on price.

On January 19, 1997, we announced the deal. We would pay $7.3 billion in Banc One stock to acquire First USA, our largest acquisition to date. (By the time the deal closed in June, the price was $7.9 billion, based on the higher value of our stock.) Combining First USA's $22.4 billion in outstanding loans with our $12.7 billion card business, we instantly became one of the top three companies in the industry, providing credit cards to thirty-two million people. That consultant sure was on to something.

At the time Banc One was the nation's tenth largest bank, with $90 billion in assets and more than 1,500 offices in thirteen states, and the First USA transaction would push us over the $100 billion mark. More importantly, we were one of the most profitable banks in the country, earning record profits of $1.4 billion in 1996.

What was so exciting about First USA was the potential for getting even more out of our existing card business. Our card business was growing at twelve percent per year while First USA was growing at twenty-five percent. In fact, First USA had the card industry's best five-year compound annual growth rate in earnings.

The reaction on Wall Street to the First USA acquisition was generally positive. Investors were well aware that First USA was a gem and agreed with us that it would be transformative for our existing card business. But there was considerable grumbling about how much we had paid. Wall Street didn't think First USA could continue to grow at its current pace. I was confident the card business could, but only time would tell.

In June we issued a press release announcing the closing of the deal, meaning it had received all necessary approvals from shareholders and passed any regulatory scrutiny. This brief and routine announcement quoted several of us, including Tolleson and myself, commenting in generalities on the deal and its prospects for success. These are usually forgettable documents, largely ignored by the public and press. But with the benefit of hindsight, this one contained some comments attributed to Dick Vague that turned out to be quite prophetic. A psychic might have foreseen trouble, though I did not at the time.

"A *top priority is to drive growth and earnings* and to achieve the economies of scale made possible by our new combined size," he said. "Both organizations possess a wealth of experience and knowledge that *we intend to aggressively apply* to our combined customer base. … Our management team recognizes the long-term opportunities that will result from combining our two organizations. We're very excited and *look forward with great commitment to seeing those opportunities maximized.*"

As I would learn, he meant it in spades.

For the remainder of 1997 and into 1998, we had plenty of work to do integrating our card operations with those of First USA. On the corporate level, we continued to implement our centralization strategy, which changed the way lines of business and authority were organized. While in the past Banc One left lots of power and decision-making in the hands of local and regional officials, all major lines of business were now organized on a national basis.

In 1998, most of these businesses reported directly to me. The people running these lines were called my direct reports. These executives oversaw our 1,500 retail branches, commercial lending and investment management activities, to name several.

One of my direct reports was Banc One President Rich Lehmann, a seasoned banker and former chairman and CEO of Valley National Bank in Arizona. Dick Vague and the card business reported to Lehmann, and not to me.

Why did we delegate in this fashion? Most CEOs at major corporations have a relatively small fixed number of direct reports, say, half a dozen, and our system was (and is) typical of large corporations. No CEO can have every department head reporting through him or her; there's simply not enough time in the day. Did you ever count the number of Assistant Secretaries in the U.S. State Department? They all report to the Secretary of State. It's a big world out there!

I trusted Lehmann to handle a variety of management tasks, and absolutely relied on him to keep me abreast of important developments at First USA and all the lines of business reporting through him. That's how the chain of command works.

CHAPTER NINETEEN

First Chicago NBD

In early 1998 none of us at Banc One was seriously thinking about another major acquisition, but that doesn't mean others weren't thinking of us. Bill Boardman routinely heard from a variety of investment bankers and other industry sources as a matter of course. Dealmakers cast a wide net and are always talking to their peers about who might be buying what or what companies are for sale.

A senior investment banker with Goldman Sachs called Bill one February morning. These guys were friends and spoke often. Ken said he had some interesting information about First Chicago NBD.

"I believe I've heard of them," Bill responded in his deadpan style, belying the slight rush of adrenalin he always felt in these situations. Of course, everyone in the industry had heard of First Chicago, the nation's ninth-largest bank with $114 billion in assets, 650 branches and fourteen international offices. This prestigious Midwestern bank was the product of the 1995 merger of First Chicago and Detroit-based NBD, the deal that nearly broke my heart.

"I wanted to make you aware of the situation up there, as I understand it," the banker continued. There was a feeling among some board members, he explained, that CEO Verne Istock, who had come from NBD and was now running the combined companies, "might not be the guy to run the bank long term."

Bill straightened in his chair. It was no secret that the merger between First Chicago and NBD had not gone as well as expected. One problem was that Istock and other senior managers never made the hard choices about consolidating operations and eliminating overlap that would have yielded cost savings and made the combination a success. Because they had failed to do that, their jobs were in jeopardy and First Chicago—as big as it was—was vulnerable to a hostile bid. And hostile bids can decimate a target company's ranks and result in the loss of a corporate headquarters.

With all this at stake, the board—primarily the dominant First Chicago faction—was questioning whether Istock—the NBD guy—was their man. One board member in particular—former First Chicago CEO Dick Thomas who was a great friend of my father's—was convinced that I was the right guy for the job. He was a strong advocate for a merger with Banc One with me at the helm.

That's how boards work, and hiring and sometimes firing the CEO is any board's number one task at hand.

Even before the merger with NBD, First Chicago had a reputation for management infighting and a long history of underperformance, lurching from one crisis and embarrassing situation to another. In 1977 one million dollares was stolen from a bank vault during a holiday weekend, money that was never recov-

◄ *Previous page:* First Chicago NBD was a prize but it came at the price of moving our headquarters. I frequently returned to Columbus for speaking engagements like this one at the Columbus Metropolitan Club.

ered. A misguided three dollar fee on customers who wanted to use tellers made the bank the butt of late-night television jokes. And in the 1980s, First Chicago had to write off more than $600 million in bad loans to developing countries.

You might be wondering why a Midwest bank would want to make loans in Chad or Bolivia. Well, remember how the restrictive banking laws in Indiana had limited branching to a single county, permanently stunting the growth of the state's banks? In Illinois, even more restrictive state laws allowed no more than a single branch, period. So if a Chicago bank was going to grow, it had to look elsewhere for business.

Meanwhile, the bank's executive suite could have been fitted with a revolving door. Chairman and CEO A. Robert Abboud left in 1985 after a five-year run, largely due to those bad foreign loans (and a bad temper to boot), followed by Barry Sullivan, a former Chase executive who was undone by bad publicity (and legal charges) surrounding a college betting pool that was being run out of his office. To make matters worse, Sullivan never moved permanently to Chicago, a constant source of irritation for the locals.

To a casual observer, Ken's comments might have seemed like routine industry gossip. But Bill knew better. Subtlety is the name of the game, and no investment banker worth his or her salt wants to portray the client as desperate for a sale or somehow damaged goods.

To Bill's trained ear, Ken's message came through loud and clear, probably with exclamation points and flashing neon lights: First Chicago was in play, and Banc One should take a serious look.

I mentioned that we still had plenty of work to do in integrating First USA, our largest acquisition ever, and weren't necessarily looking to swallow another big fish. But in banking M&A, you have to be ready to move when opportunity knocks, and the tap on the door might come while you're still digesting your last meal. When you have the chance to buy a great company, you act, and this was an opportunity beating down our door.

Bill was in my office within seconds of hanging up the phone. There was no question we were interested in First Chicago NBD, which would be such a logical combination with Banc One from a geographical and product line standpoint. Culturally, we were different, but not that different.

"The name of the company can be Banc One, but they insist that the headquarters be in Chicago," Bill said.

We paused and looked at each other briefly, but neither of us was all that surprised. We had already been down this road when we flirted with the PNC transaction and possibly moving the headquarters to Pittsburgh. We agreed then that we would consider moving if it meant a meaningful acquisition, or if it was in a location that could make a difference to us. In this case, we felt Chicago offered both.

From a recruitment and talent aspect alone, it's generally easier to try to convince a senior executive to come to Chicago than to Columbus or Pittsburgh. Chicago is not only a financial center, but it's a cultural and transportation hub. It's easier to move around the country and the world from Chicago than from other cities in the Midwest. This is no knock against Columbus or Minneapolis, but these are the facts.

The first order of business was a get-acquainted meeting. Bill arranged for us to meet in Chicago with Verne and his chief financial officer, Bob Rosholt. At this point you might be wondering what Verne thought was happening. My feeling was he was aware of the lack of confidence among key board members, who after all had engaged Goldman Sachs to put out feelers about alternatives. So my presumption was that Verne was being a good soldier and prepared to discuss a merger resulting in his transitioning to a new role, i.e., no longer CEO.

Verne (who was 57 at the time to my 54) was a University of Michigan graduate who joined the National Bank of Detroit as a credit analyst right out of graduate school in 1963. In 1994, he was named chairman and CEO of NBD Bancorp, and a year later helped Dick Thomas, CEO of First Chicago, and Chick Fisher, chairman of NBD, negotiate the merger of NBD and First Chicago. The deal called for Verne ending up as CEO of the combined companies. Verne may not have been the best operator or most admired banker in the industry, but he was skilled at office politics and sure had a knack for landing on top.

The actual negotiations weren't difficult, probably because both sides agreed to four major components at the outset: 1. it would be a merger of equals; 2. I would be president and CEO (effectively running the company) while Verne would be chairman (running board meetings); 3. the name of the company would be Bank One Corp., and 4. the headquarters would be in Chicago.

Of all the conditions, I think Verne was most surprised that we agreed without a fight or concession to relocate to Chicago. That was a huge matter of pride for them. It would have been a tremendous blow to egos if First Chicago would be run from Columbus as Bank One. It would have pretty much ended their corporate bloodline.

For us, Chicago made perfect sense, though of course that feeling wasn't universally shared by the Columbus business community and many of our employees. I was never forgiven by the publisher of *The Columbus Dispatch* at that time, John F. Wolfe, a former high school classmate. Ironically, his family had sold their formerly family-controlled bank in Columbus, BancOhio, to Cleveland-based National City (now PNC), and later sold his family owned, Columbus-based retail brokerage, The Ohio Company, to Cincinnati-based Fifth Third Bank. His newspaper never mentioned *that* in the editorials excoriating me for giving up local control of the bank.

That leaves the merger of equals part. What exactly is a merger of equals?

Most of the banks we acquired were no more than twenty percent of our size based on assets, and there was no question that Banc One was the buyer and surviving entity. That's what you call a traditional acquisition. But in banking, when two similar-sized banks joined forces, there was more give and take in how things were combined and who was running the show.

From a size and stature standpoint, Banc One and First Chicago were very equivalent, although we were slightly larger by assets, had more than twice as many branches and were considerably more profitable. They did have a larger national and international commercial lending business, a good credit card company and the dominant retail-banking position in Illinois, where we had 4 percent of deposits, and Michigan, where we had a very small presence.

Usually, when we bought a bank we paid a premium of twenty percent to thirty percent. But in a merger of equals scenario, the premium goes way down. And in this case it was close to zero, because their profitability didn't command any premium. So we saved our shareholders a considerable amount of equity. Finally, we agreed to have equal board representation—eleven members from each company—another sign that this was more of a combination than a conquest.

With those major decisions out of the way, both sides agreed to negotiate who would run the combined lines of business, and who they would report through. Usually this process occurred after a deal had closed, but it can be a messy and time-consuming process, so we wanted to tackle it early on.

Once again, Bill and I sat down with Verne and CFO Bob Rosholt. When the smoke had cleared, we decided that most operating divisions would report to or through me, and most support divisions would report to or through Verne. Operating divisions make money and include retail branches and consumer lending, credit cards, investment management and consumer finance/mortgage lending. Support divisions generally costs a company money and include legal, human resources, public relations and finance departments.

So I was comfortable that I was running the bank, and Bill and I were quite pleased that we were able to place so many senior Banc One managers in leadership positions. Eighteen months later, however, when controversy surrounding First USA split our board into warring factions, I would come to regret not having more of my allies in offices including legal, PR, HR and finance. More on that later.

On Monday April 13, 1998, Verne and I shared a podium at New York's Waldorf-Astoria to announce the $29 billion merger of equals between Banc One and First Chicago NBD, creating Chicago-based Bank One Corporation (yes, no more 'Banc').

Six weeks of negotiations had produced the nation's sixth-largest bank with 90,000 employees, assets of $230 billion and 1,950 branches in thirteen states. Together we held four percent of the country's bank deposits. The combination also made Bank One the nation's largest issuer of credit cards, a highly profitable business when done right.

Our deal was the third-largest banking merger ever, trailing the $80 billion combination of Citicorp and Travelers Group, announced one week earlier, and another one announced the same day as ours—and in the same hotel no less!—creating the largest U.S. bank through the $59.3 billion merger of BankAmerica and NationsBank. Yes, there was no standing still in bank M&A back then.

To get Justice Department antitrust approval, we did agree to divest 39 branches in Indiana with deposits of nearly $1.5 billion, and to sell some commercial loans in Indiana, to avoid too much market concentration.

Back home, the news didn't go over so well. Banc One was a homegrown business, the largest corporation in town and possibly the best known (Wendy's, Nationwide Insurance and the former Limited Brands and its Victoria's Secret might have something to say about that). Losing a leading corporate citizen hurts, and I can understand the concerns.

But we had 9,500 employees in Columbus when the deal was announced, and they weren't going anywhere. I pledged that there would be more a year later, and that promise was kept. Columbus remains a major employment hub for JPMorgan Chase, in a facility we built that is named for John G. McCoy. At 2 million square feet, the McCoy Center is the second largest "flat" office building (as opposed to an office tower) in the nation after the Pentagon. As of this writing there are more than 25,000 Chase employees in Columbus— more than any private company and trailing only the State of Ohio and Ohio State University—something I'm very proud of.

By the summer of 1998, it was time for Bank One brass to relocate. Joining me in Chicago was a number of senior executives, including Bill Boardman. Another was Rich Lehmann, our president, who would become one of two vice chairmen along with David Vitale from First Chicago. I was very excited to be moving to Chicago, as was Jane. Our kids were grown and out of the house and we were looking forward to a new adventure together.

Bill, Rich and I arrived from Columbus on the same day to settle into our new offices, sharing an executive floor with Vern, Vitale and Rosholt. Verne and I were on opposite ends of the floor while Bill and I were next-door neighbors, just as we had always been in Columbus.

On the first day, a Monday, we were invited to a meeting with Verne and his folks. There was nothing pressing on the agenda, just an initial get-together as a new management team with lots of new personalities and tasks at hand. We had to start somewhere, and this was the beginning.

Having stopped at a coffee station on our way to the meeting, Bill, Rich and I were each holding our Styrofoam cups as we entered the executive board room. Verne was seated at the head of a dark wooden table with the others on either side of him. He locked onto us just inside the doorway.

"Uh, we don't drink coffee in this room," Verne said sternly with a scowl on his face.

The three of us froze, some in mid-sip, as our brains processed the rebuke. It was as if we had walked onto a freshly waxed floor with muddy shoes and were hearing it from mom.

We sheepishly placed our cups on the nearest side-table and muttered our apologies. Then we took our seats around the table.

The meeting went on as planned and nothing more was said about the coffee, but it was an awkward way to start our working relationship. With the benefit of hindsight, the episode should have served as a warning that these folks weren't playing by the same rules as we were, and we weren't in Kansas (or Columbus) anymore.

The Banc One culture in Columbus had always been a reflection of my personal management style: collaboration and collegiality were paramount, so please check your egos at the door. We were all on the same team and working toward the same goal, and the best way to get there was for everyone to be rowing in the same direction. Don't be afraid to take chances, but ask for help when things go wrong, and we'll fix it together. If you've got a problem with me, tell it to my face, and I'll do likewise. And finally, save the office drama for the Christmas play. (OK, we didn't have a Christmas play, but you get my point.)

I should have recognized something more far-reaching in Verne's admonishment. He wasn't protecting the finish on the conference room table; he was guarding his turf. His real message was, "This is my conference room and my company, and this is how we do things around here. You hayseeds need to get with the program."

I plead guilty to naiveté in regard to this type of nonsense. If I had spent much time in a highly political atmosphere such as First Chicago's, I'm sure I would have recognized Verne's comment for what it was: a challenge to my authority. I wasn't prepared for the pettiness.

Years later, Bill remarked that what I should have done when Verne said, "We don't drink coffee in this room," was to stroll right in and say, "Well, that just changed. We do from now on and you're gonna love it. We're gonna get some great coffee." We all wish we could hit the rewind button at times, and this was one of those moments.

Just what type of workplace environment had we entered? The coffee episode was just the beginning. Over the next weeks and months the First Chicago culture would become more apparent to us, as did the realization that bridging the cultural gap would be more difficult than we anticipated.

(An observation here about Chicagoans and their beloved city: they are intensely loyal to what is a great town, but they can be awfully parochial for big-city folks. As chronicled in the novel, *The Devil in the White City*, Chicagoans have long harbored an inferiority complex as it relates to their larger and maybe more cosmopolitan rival, New York. Chafing from this "Second City" status, some Chicagoans feel a need to be recognized as the cultural avatars of the Midwest, if nowhere else, and can go to great lengths to let anyone from Milwaukee or Detroit or, God forbid, Columbus, Ohio, know this in no uncertain terms.)

Generally, it took two years after an acquisition to make an acquired company part of us. How did it happen? The new company took our name and branding and started selling our products. They now had access to all kinds of customer support and career-advancement opportunities that a larger organization could provide. And when market share increased and profits rose, many of them shared in the spoils.

First Chicago did take our name and branding, but to some of their people it felt like a hair shirt. Big city pride definitely played a part. There was lingering resentment that this old-line, namesake company had been taken over by perceived provincials fixin' to wipe their muddy boots on the executive dining room carpet. Though they needed our investment and expertise to restore luster to a faded brand, they still woke up every morning hoping it was all a bad dream and that we'd be gone.

Many months into our move, Bill mentioned to a Chicago acquaintance that he was surprised that no First Chicago folks had invited him out for a drink or offered to sponsor him for a club membership—routine events when new executives came to town in Columbus. The friend looked at him and said, very matter of factly: "Don't you know? They don't want you here."

The cold shoulder extended beyond the office. Mayor Richard Daley shot down plans for a ten-foot Bank One sign atop First Chicago's former fifty-seven-story headquarters. *Chicago Tribune* columnist Ellen Warren belittled our plans in two critical columns with more than a little arrogance.

"It was my view that we don't need to label our skyscrapers with the names of crappy companies," she later told *The Columbus Dispatch*. "Labeling tall buildings is worthy of places like Columbus."

This is not to say that we weren't making progress in combining the operations of Banc One and First Chicago. We were. By July 1999, I was comfortable that things were coming together in the timeframe I expected. The vast majority of our employees, regardless of what camp they came from, were working well together, despite the continued coolness toward us in upper-management ranks. Did we have a lot of work to do? Yes, this was a very big enterprise with lots of moving parts. But overall, the world was good.

CHAPTER TWENTY

Trouble in Card Paradise

In early July, I got a phone call from Dick Vague at First USA. "John, we've got a problem."

I can't say that I was surprised because I'd heard that before. Vague was a little like the boy who cried wolf in meeting financial goals. At the start of every quarter he would say, "We're not going to make our numbers this quarter," for any variety of reasons. The economy was weak or people were carrying smaller balances or the competition was really aggressive—it was always something.

Yet despite protestations, First USA was always able to meet the aggressive financial goals we set. And these were very big numbers—First USA earned $1 billion in 1998, one third of the entire company's total. Yes, it was a fantastic business, but that's how we were able to justify the premium we had paid for it.

There was always an underlying tension between senior corporate management and First USA brass about making the numbers, but that was not necessarily unusual or unique to that line of business. We set aggressive targets for all our divisions, and with rare exceptions most of them operated superbly and reached their goals every quarter. And it was always a bigger number.

"What is it, Dick?" I asked, sitting back and gazing out toward Lake Michigan, shimmering in the morning sun.

"John, we're only going to make $200 million this quarter."

Now that would be a *real* problem. If I had been standing up at the time I might gone a bit wobbly.

"You're saying what?"

"That we're going to have a significant shortfall this quarter."

Bad news of this magnitude can take a few seconds to sink in. My initial thought was how could something this big happen so quickly? A business that pulls in nearly $250 million a quarter on a regular basis doesn't all of a sudden earn $50 million less in the space of three months. At least no business that I had ever been associated with. It just wasn't adding up.

"Hang on," I replied. "How can you only make $200 million this quarter?"

He paused, then said, "I'm not really sure we got that figured out."

By now my patience was wearing a little thin. I wanted answers and Vague was talking nonsense as far as I was concerned. I believed he was holding something back.

"Well, we're gonna need to get to the bottom of it and get it fixed fast," I said, or words to that effect. And that was basically the bottom line. When things don't go right in business, first you identify the problem, then you get it fixed. Pronto.

But was Vague the guy to figure it out? It sure didn't sound like it. Here was the founder of an extremely successful business telling me we were going

◄ *Previous page:* Financial shortfalls at First USA dominated the news pages in 1999 and contributed to infighting that would eventually divide the Bank One board.

to have a significant shortfall in the space of several months and he wasn't sure why. That kind of statement does not breed confidence. There was an element of unreality about the whole situation.

"Don't worry, we'll get it fixed," he assured me.

When I got off the phone with Vague, who was at First USA's headquarters in Delaware, I immediately set out to find Rich Lehmann, whose office was down the hall. Recall that Vague reported to Lehmann, who in turn reported to me. That was our chain of command, so if there was any kind of problem at First USA, Lehmann ought to be aware of it. Hopefully he could fill me in.

Lehmann was just as surprised as I was to hear about a shortfall at First USA. Now I'm really concerned. As a former bank chairman and CEO, Lehmann was quite capable of identifying a bad trend or unwise practice before things got out of hand. Rich had spent twenty years as an executive with Citicorp before taking the helm at Valley National in Arizona. This was no management trainee. But here he was, informing me that he wasn't aware of any issues at First USA, a line of business that reported directly to him.

Even worse than any shortfall, as far as I was concerned, was that our lines and communication were not functioning. I relied on Lehmann to be my eyes and ears with every business that reported to him. As a major profit center, First USA should have been at the forefront. But Lehmann was in the dark.

However we had gotten into this predicament, First USA's problem was undeniably mine. I may not have known how big it was or what caused it, but it was sitting right in my lap. What I needed most was the facts. If your doctor says you have a tumor, you have to know where it's located, how big it is and whether it's malignant before you start any treatment. Likewise, we had to understand our problem in the shortest amount of time, or no fix was possible.

Disclosure was a major issue to consider. Public companies have a legal obligation to disclose material developments to their shareholders and the entire investment community, and this large of an earnings shortfall was about as material as you could get. If we were making that much less money in such a short timeframe, the result would be a significantly lower stock valuation. So someone buying Banc One stock at pre-disclosure prices would be awfully mad, and rightly so, if the stock lost a third of its value a week later.

That's one reason why large public companies keep in regular contact with the Wall Street analysts who in turn recommend to investors whether to buy or sell a company's stock. The idea is to "guide" analysts with earnings expectations, giving them a sense of how your business is doing so they in turn can project what valuation your stock deserves.

Nobody wants to buy a $100 stock with the expectation that it will earn ten dollars a share when in reality the company is about to shock the world with earnings of five dollars a share. Earnings guidance helps keep stock prices and expectations in line with reality, thereby eliminating wild swings in the market.

An earnings shortfall is one thing, but an *unexpected* earnings shortfall is quite another. Wall Street hates surprises more than anything else, so we would need to move quickly to disclose what we knew ahead of our next quarterly earnings report. Our reputation was at stake, as well as the value of our shareholders' investments. But at least for now, we had nothing to disclose because we didn't understand the scope of the problem. That's about the worst predicament for a CEO to be in, and one I wasn't accustomed to.

Because both Vague and Lehmann had expressed ignorance, I sent Bill Boardman to Delaware to get to the bottom of things. Bill was a numbers guy who understood the intricacies of a balance sheet and how a business should be run. Ultimately, it would take us more than three months to get the whole picture, but by late August—a little more than halfway through the third quarter—we felt we knew enough to go public with our findings.

What we had learned after a closer look at First USA was that it wasn't one thing, it was multiple things. A number of small, misguided decisions had built up to a crescendo with disastrous results.

The first bad decision in this chain of events was shortening by one day the grace period for First USA customers to pay their bills. It had always been thirty days, but Vague's folks quietly reduced the grace period by a day, with the intended result of more payments being late and more customers being charged a thirty dollar late fee. (These were the days before widespread use of electronic payments, so people needed time to write a check and send their payment through the mail.) In addition to the late fee, the reduced grace period allowed the bank to charge one more day of interest, and that was probably a larger number than the late fee.

Not a very nice thing to do, perhaps, but what if it meant an additional $250 million a year in profits for First USA? That must have looked like low-hanging fruit to some people at First USA.

Not surprisingly, the late fees and higher interest charges resulted in an uptick in customer complaints. Not an avalanche at first, but a noticeable increase if anyone cared to take notice. A few months later, a second day was chopped off the grace period, which resulted in more fees, interest, and customer complaints. Then a third day was eliminated—you get the picture.

As the protests increased, there weren't enough employees to handle the call volume, so customers got even madder and lodged complaints with the Office of the Comptroller of the Currency (OCC), a federal oversight agency regulating all national banks and thrifts.

Customers were defecting, so management began to pull other levers to compensate. Instead of accepting new accounts with credit scores of 650, they accepted 640, then 630, then 620. They raised and lowered interest rates, angering long-time customers who could take their business to our competitors, which they did.

First USA had lost control. Like a frantic Wizard of Oz, Vague had a lot of levers he could pull, and he was yanking on them all. This combination of shortcuts and near-term Band-Aids damaged the brand and drove away customers. Our "surprise" earnings shortfall should have been anticipated and dealt with many months in advance, when something could have been done about it.

So who should have seen it coming? Vague certainly, because he was that man behind the curtain making so many bad business decisions. He knew exactly what was happening, but not why. And of course Lehmann, who was responsible for the First USA business and should have been visiting Delaware on a regular basis, reviewing trends and financials with Vague, and being close enough to the business to sniff out early warning signs such as rising customer complaints and attrition.

An alert chief financial officer also should spot trouble on a grand scale. The CFO is constantly taking the financial pulse of a corporation, and should see upward or downward trends in a matter of weeks if not days. Did Bob Rosholt, a First Chicago carryover, have my back in this crucial role? Maybe not.

And of course me. While I can say that I was let down by trusted deputies who should have known better, the CEO is ultimately responsible for all aspects of the business. I was the sheriff who chose those deputies and should have realized that Vague was a loose cannon and Lehmann wasn't on top of the situation at First USA. Lehmann was an excellent banker who helped us in many situations, and we remain friends to this day, but he was not nearly as vigilant as he needed to be in this matter, something he has acknowledged to me many times and still feels terrible about.

In a sense, all of us at Bank One had let our guard down with First USA to some extent. These folks were the recognized leaders in the card industry and we viewed them as the saviors of our decent but not great card business. I was comfortable in letting them run things their way so long as the results were good, which they always had been.

But here was a critical mistake on my part: We ceded too much operational control to folks in another state that we did not know so well. In retrospect, we erred in not moving some of our trusted financial people, steeped in the Bank One way of doing things, to Delaware to oversee and integrate the First USA business. We always did that with banks that we acquired—because we were the recognized leaders in banking—and should have done so with First USA. That might have kept them from taking shortcuts or at least revealed these issues before they got out of hand.

Also in hindsight, the loss of First USA co-founder Tolleson as a guiding light was catastrophic. Before the acquisition, the way they functioned as a team was something like this: Vague would come up with twenty ideas a week and Tolleson would kill eighteen of them. He was the voice of reason balancing Vague's creative and often brilliant impulses. We didn't appreciate how important this dynamic was for the business.

After the acquisition, Tolleson had removed himself from direct involvement in First USA to take a seat on our board. I had hoped that he would continue to play a meaningful advisory role at First USA, but I now understood that the loss of his steady hand had unleashed Vague in unhealthy ways. Lehmann had not filled Tolleson's former role, and I was one step removed from the day-to-day. It was a prescription for disaster and I paid a very steep price for that.

Here's how the chain of command should have worked with a major decision at First USA or any line of business: Dick Vague or Rich Lehmann comes to me and says, "John, we'd like to reduce the billing grace period by a day to generate late fees and additional income." And I would have either said no, or at least let them try to convince me that it would have no negative impact on the business. And (most likely) then said no. But I never had that opportunity, and it's something that still frustrates me.

On Tuesday August 24, 1999, we made an announcement after the markets had closed that our earnings for the second half of the year would be $530 million below expectations. The following day we held a meeting with analysts, at New York's Waldorf-Astoria, to go over the details and answer their questions.

Our revised estimate for operating earnings for 1999 was between $3.60 and $3.65 a share, eight percent below the $3.92 a share that Wall Street had been expecting. (In November, as we more fully understood the depths of our problem, we would reduce that even further, to a range of $3.45 to $3.55 a share.) Not surprisingly, our stock plunged 23 percent in heavy trading the day we disclosed our problems at First USA. Wall Street and investors had every right to be disappointed.

A *Wall Street Journal* reporter said our announcement "amounted to an admission that the slower growth rate of the mature banking industry has caught up with the company," and "made clear that investors won't soon see the promised benefits of Bank One's merger last year with First Chicago NBD."

The same article quoted a leading analyst as saying, "For a lot of investors, things have changed, because the company they thought they had is different than the company they have today."

There was no arguing the point.

Far more damaging than any short-term earnings miss was the impact on our corporate culture and integration efforts. By August 1999, just before the First USA controversy, we were a little over a year into the First Chicago merger and well on the way to becoming one company. After August 24, all that progress was undone. In a nutshell, the issues at First USA were seen as a Bank One problem, not a First Chicago problem. The perception was that our side had screwed up, and that powerful dynamic served to divide the company—and especially the board—into warring camps.

Our directors were upset, their directors were upset, and everyone had a right to be. The main difference was that the former Banc One directors were willing to let me get to the bottom of it, while the First Chicago/NBD directors also wanted me to get to the bottom—of Lake Michigan in cement boots!

One of the first actions the board took was to give Verne a wider operational role. While I retained the CEO title and direct responsibility for First USA, Verne was named president and given responsibility for the other lines of business that had reported through Lehmann. It was a rebuke to me.

Verne saw opportunity in the turmoil. As you recall, he had requested that the chief legal counsel, human resources chief and public relations director all report through him. At Verne's insistence, we also had retained First Chicago's chief financial officer, Rosholt. Those choices seemed odd to me at the time, because these were not the profit-generating portions of the bank. I was pleased to have my people in leadership positions in retail banking, consumer lending and other major lines of business. But in times of crisis, having allies in finance, human resources, legal and public relations roles proved to be an asset for Verne and a liability for me.

Here's why: A chief financial officer mans the front lines opposite the investment community, and plays a leading role in managing the expectations of Wall Street. In times of crisis, a skilled and loyal CFO can deflect a fair amount of heat from the CEO by keeping a cool head.

Likewise, a company's chief legal counsel is an important advisor in times of crisis, especially in devising a plan for disclosing financially sensitive information. In addition, the chief legal counsel serves as a liaison to outside law firms that may be called upon by the board or senior executives for a variety of reasons, including M&A and leadership changes. A trusted legal advisor is every CEO's best friend in difficult times.

Finally, controlling the messaging at a large corporation is a complex process under normal circumstances. Relationships with local and national media, not to mention communication within the company itself, all play a part in how a company and those running it are perceived. A bad PR team, or one not in step with the CEO, is a real liability.

I took a beating in the Chicago press in the immediate aftermath of the First USA disclosures—some of it justified, some of it not. In particular, I was subject to several negative stories for going on a family vacation to Europe for one week, leaving a few days after the First USA disclosure. Granted, it was not ideal timing, but my feeling was it was a long planned trip, I was in constant communication with the office, and there was not much I could do about First USA until Boardman figured out the issues.

Another spate of negative stories appeared in the Chicago papers a month later, when I traveled to Dallas for the Bank One Senior Championship. This would have been on my calendar for a year, and there was no question in my mind that the CEO of Bank One needed to be at the Bank One Senior Championship.

Not only was it a nationally televised golf tournament, but this was a multi-day networking event attended by our very best customers and several dozen CEOs of Fortune 500 companies. Yes, playing golf was a big part of the activities, but so was a formal dinner with a keynote speaker, who I was seated next to at the head table. My approach was we had to keep running this business whether or not we had a problem at First USA. Holing up in a bunker wasn't the answer.

I had it on good authority that Verne's communications people were approaching Chicago journalists with damaging information about me. To make matters worse, our communications chief, Gerald Buldak, who reported to Verne, started compiling these press clips and sending them out to board members on a regular basis. Most of the stories were critical of Bank One or me specifically, which is the opposite of what you might expect from a company's communications team. I believe this was part of an orchestrated effort, spearheaded by Verne, to further weaken my position.

First USA ended up losing 1.1 million customers in the third quarter, which ended September 30. By October, Bill was making sufficient progress in piecing together the problems at First USA that I felt it was time to part ways with Vague and Lehmann. Lehmann absolutely understood that he had to go, and was very apologetic and even emotional as we met to set a retirement date for him the following month. He was fifty-five at the time.

True to form, Vague, then forty-two, was incredulous that he was being let go. We met for dinner in a private room of the Chicago Club, and when I gave him the news that we had to part ways, he walked out. I was not surprised. (A little less than a year later Vague hired a publicist to spread the word that he had been unjustly scapegoated for problems at First USA and that he was vindicated by my departure from the bank.)

As the year wound down our earnings outlook was reduced a second time, and the board grew increasingly divided. It didn't help that we had to postpone a November 15 investor update because we still had not completed our internal reviews of First USA. Gratefully, the twelve former Banc One board members, led by my long-time friend and colleague Bob Walter, who was founder and CEO of the healthcare products and distribution company

Cardinal Health, remained behind me. But the First Chicago/NBD faction, which had been reduced to eleven members with the voluntary departure of Vice Chairman Vitale (effective November 1), was in open revolt. The situation was coming to a head.

John Bryan (CEO of Sara Lee) and Dick Manoogian (CEO of Masco), representing the First Chicago faction, asked for a private meeting with Walter and John Hall, directors from our side. The meeting was held at the Columbus Club, an elegant downtown social club across the street from our former Banc One headquarters, and Bryan was none too happy about having to trek to Columbus. He, of course, expected the proceedings to be in Chicago.

Bryan and Manoogian, who was from Detroit, demanded that I be fired. Bob and John argued that I deserved more time to turn things around, and reminded them that the old Banc One side still had the votes. Our side prevailed, but this was obviously not a healthy development.

These were trying times for all of us professionally, and for me personally, as you can imagine. I'm not combative by nature. I won't walk away from a fight, mind you, but I will always seek common ground.

Office intrigue and politics of the sort being played out was anathema to me. What was best for the company came ahead of any aspirations or ego on my part. I was growing weary of the bickering and very concerned the company could be damaged if it continued much longer. My heart still goes out to the thousands of Bank One employees who lived through that turmoil.

Jane and I spent many hours on the balcony of our Chicago apartment discussing the situation and considering all the options. She has always been such a great sounding board for me in business and other matters, bringing her enlightened outsider's view to any situation. During these balcony talks she even put up with my occasional cigar smoking, which she absolutely hates but was kind enough to tolerate.

With Lehmann and Vague gone, I needed management talent to help me through this rough patch, and maybe—just maybe—become my replacement should things not work out for me. I was more convinced than ever that Verne didn't have the skills, temperament or character to run the company.

And I have to believe that the First Chicago faction felt much the same way about Verne. After all, the reason First Chicago was willing to do the merger with us in the first place was that a majority on their board did not believe Verne was the right person to lead that company to prosperity. So while it was easy, post-merger, for them to rail against McCoy and First USA, they ultimately called their own bluff by never advocating whole-heartedly for Verne.

"Bank One doesn't have enough bench to accommodate this change," Chicago-based executive recruiter Peter Crist was quoted as saying about our executive purge in a November article in *Investment News*. "They've created a very complex model with a lot of moving parts. It requires some very high-level human talent—and a lot of it." I couldn't argue with that.

CHAPTER TWENTY-ONE

'Jamie is your guy'

Judi Rosen was a management consultant who had worked for me in Columbus and Chicago. Judi had helped streamline our management structure at the old Banc One when we were transitioning from the decentralized "uncommon partnership" system, and later played a role in combining management teams at Banc One and First Chicago. Her instincts about people and ability to judge talent were impressive. We hired Judi full time after the move to Chicago.

Judi knew lots of people in all kinds of management positions. She was a former Harvard Business School classmate with Jamie Dimon, a talented but brash young banking executive who had worked with Sandy Weill at American Express and then followed him to Commercial Credit. With skillful acquisitions, Weill and Dimon built Commercial Credit into the insurance and financial services conglomerate Travelers Group. In 1998, Travelers merged with Citicorp, run by my good friend John Reed, in an $83 billion transaction.

Weill and Reed were co-chairmen and co-CEOs for 18 months, and during that time, Dimon reported to Reed on the banking side of the company. Their personalities were very different and they frequently clashed. During one of their arguments over how to handle something, Reed settled things by saying, "I'm the CEO, and this is what we're going to do." Reed was frustrated enough that he went to Weill and encouraged him to fire Dimon, which is just what Weill did in November 1998.

With Dimon out of a job and with me on a management island, Rosen encouraged me to think about bringing him to Bank One as my deputy. "John, you need talent," Judi said to me. "Jamie Dimon is your guy."

I had never met Jamie, who was living in New York, and knew only what I had read about him. By all accounts he was smart. I trusted Judi, who had spent a full year with him at Harvard and then kept in touch tangentially through the ensuing years. (I was concerned at the time that if this guy was so good, why did he get fired? I ended up speaking to John Reed about him, and Reed confirmed that it was not a question of talent or character, but more about the internal dynamics at Citi that proved to be Jamie's undoing there.) Serving as a go-between, Judi reached out to Jamie on my behalf. Would he be interested in talking to John McCoy about a role at Bank One? Absolutely, he informed her.

Toward the end of November I followed up with a call, in which I introduced myself and sketched out some of the issues I was facing back in Chicago. "Jamie, I'm sure you've read about what's going on," I began. "I've had to fire two top people in the company, and I need more leadership. I'd like to talk to you about it to see whether there's a fit between us."

◄ *Previous page:* Jamie Dimon *(left)*, a talented banker whom I identified as a possible successor, was ultimately hired as CEO after I retired. This picture, with me on the right, was taken by my sister, Jinny, at John G.'s 90th birthday party.

Of course he had been following developments in the newspapers and he could also read between the lines. I could tell right away that he grasped the situation and was very interested in what was going on. We spoke for about ten minutes and agreed to meet later that week when I would be in New York on business.

"Thanks for thinking of me John," he said. "I'm looking forward to having a meeting."

Jamie came to my suite in the Carlyle Hotel on the Upper East Side. He was dressed in a coat and tie and looked every inch the competent executive that he was purported to be. We exchanged some pleasantries and he talked about what he had been doing for the past six months since being fired from Citi—taking time off to think. He'd also spent quite a bit of time in Europe with his family.

So then I asked him what he wanted to do with the rest of his life. After all, the guy was very youthful, roughly thirteen years my junior, and had his whole career ahead of him.

"I could do three things," he began, obviously having thought it through. "I could be an investment banker; I could be a merchant banker; or I could go back into commercial banking and show that S.O.B. (Weill) just how good I am!" We both laughed. Vintage Jamie Dimon, I would come to learn.

I liked the guy right away. We were obviously different in temperament, but he possessed three things I was in dire need of—energy, passion and most of all, talent. Always in my career, as Bank One grew, we had to continuously go outside searching for talent. Here was a man who had helped build Commercial Credit and had been at Citicorp. He knew a lot of people in the business and could refresh our management ranks because of those connections. I had the feeling that if he came to Bank One he could recruit a ton of talent.

I explained to Jamie that I had just fired Rich Lehmann and Dick Vague and was in need of someone to help me run the company. He was intrigued by the possibility of coming to Bank One in a senior operational role. No formal offer was made in that first meeting, and we agreed to keep in touch.

After the meeting, I was quite convinced that there were very few banking executives of Jamie's caliber in the entire country. I was confident that he could come in as my number two and be ready to replace me in eighteen to twenty-four months—that was my working plan. It's often hard to find a number two because they usually want to be number one right away. In this case I had the feeling that he would be willing to come to Bank One if he could become CEO within two years. I came away from the meeting thinking, "I've got my guy."

Then something happened that totally changed the dynamics of the situation. On the last Sunday in November, Martin Lipton, a founding partner of our New York-based corporate law firm Wachtell, Lipton, Rosen & Katz, flew to Chicago for a secret meeting with the eleven members of the First Chicago/NBD faction of the Bank One board. Secret in the sense that neither I, the CEO of the company, nor any of the twelve board members from the pre-merger Banc One, were invited or knew anything about the gathering. Also present was Sherman Goldberg, Bank One's chief legal counsel, who was not on the board but had helped to organize the clandestine gathering.

Crown, Bryan and others on the First Chicago/NBD side were seeking Lipton's counsel on how they could get rid of their CEO—me! This was outrageous on several fronts, most notably because Wachtell Lipton represented the entire corporation and not a subset of the board. And beleaguered though I was, I remained the head of that corporation. It was clearly improper for individual board members to call upon our corporate law firm to pursue a private agenda, and even worse that Lipton had consented to take part.

After a few days I got word that something had happened. I immediately called Goldberg. "Sherm, I understand there was a meeting. What went on?"

"John, it's confidential," he replied. "I can't tell you."

That wasn't going to cut it with me.

"Sherm, who do you work for?" I inquired. "And who does Marty Lipton work for—half the board or the full board?"

"Well," he said, "I can't say."

I suspended him over the phone. "I don't want you back in this office," I said, and Sherm was done.

I telephoned Verne and got basically the same results. "I can't tell you John, it's confidential," he replied. I was not in a position to suspend Verne, and it wouldn't have done any good anyhow.

Then I dialed up Ed Herlihy, a partner at the Wachtell Lipton law firm, who was also a trusted friend.

"Eddie, I understand Marty was out here the other day, just talking to the First Chicago people, and they are plotting on what to do with me."

Herlihy was shocked. "What?" he replied. "Let me get right back to you," he said, hanging up the phone.

Half an hour later my phone rang. It was Herlihy. "Yes, Marty was there," he confirmed, "and Marty didn't appreciate that it was just half the board, that it was just First Chicago, so Marty's going to have to exclude himself from further dealings. He plans to call you to apologize."

While that gave me some satisfaction, the bigger and much more troubling issue was that the Bank One board was now in open revolt, divided into warring factions, and much of the fighting was about me.

So now I'm angry in addition to being wounded. Double dealing and backroom maneuverings were not my style, and I wanted it to end.

I called a special board meeting, which as CEO I had the authority to do, for the following Sunday. It was to be held in the Chicago office of our new attorney, Ted Tetzlaff, a real bright and tough lawyer who I had gotten to know from my work on another board on which I served. (As much as I loved Ed Herlihy, I had to get another firm to represent the company because the Wachtell Lipton firm was so compromised.)

At this juncture, the First Chicago side was feeling exposed, especially after taking the bold step of meeting in secret with Marty Lipton. What they had done was wrong—possibly worthy of disqualifying them from serving on a public board—and as the meeting approached, I think their side understood how far out on a limb they had gone.

Yet I was not thinking purge or retribution. Imagine the blow back if we had gone into that meeting and voted all the First Chicago people off the board and fired Verne. It might have felt good for about five minutes, but the reaction in the banking world and business community would have been negative. Picture this headline in the *New York Times*: "In boardroom coup, McCoy gets rid of all opposing directors and fires Istock." What would that have accomplished for our company and our stock? That's what you call a pyrrhic victory—winning a battle but losing the war.

No, I believed I had come up with something acceptable to both sides that would buy us all some time to make the fixes that needed to be made. I was determined to spend the whole day, if necessary, working through our issues.

Bob Walter and I conferred before the showdown. He knew I wanted to stand up for what was right, but he was also well aware of how tired I had grown of the infighting. I was concerned that the company was being damaged, and I strongly believed that it was my duty as CEO to put the company's interests ahead of my own.

I met with our directors the night before the special meeting, telling them I didn't plan to go to war, and that we needed to find a solution that solved our problem and ended the bickering between the two sides. Almost everybody was 100 percent supportive of finding a solution that didn't blow up the company, with the lone exception of Tolleson, who seemed open to a showdown. That probably had something to do with how the problems at First USA had triggered this crisis, and how the First Chicago faction had wielded those problems like a club to batter our side. A lot of nasty things were said about First USA in the previous five months, not all of it justified or accurate, and that was his company, after all.

The meeting was scheduled for 10 a.m. in a large, glass-enclosed boardroom in Tetzlaff's office, and directors from both sides didn't really show up until a few minutes before then. While there was tension in the room, I would not describe it as warlike. Despite months of bickering, these were all rational people and the proceedings were civil. In fact, most people said nothing or very little. You go to any board, and only two or three people are making all the decisions. On our side it was Bob Walter and on their side John Bryan. (For several months now, Walter and Bryan had been the recognized spokesmen and leaders of their respective sides. Verne and I were basically lightning rods to the opposing factions, that's where things stood.)

I had called the meeting so I started the proceedings. The format called for me to address the board, make my proposal, and then leave the room so that Verne could do the same.

"I've come up with a plan that I believe will move this company forward," I explained. "It's very simple. I propose to hire a new president to help me run the bank, and if at some point I should leave the company, then the president will become CEO." That was my way of making a major concession on my leadership without ceding power to Verne, who was absolutely not the right person to run the bank going forward.

Then I left the room and it was Verne's turn. He reminded the board that the issues at First USA were my problem and not his, and (in so many words) explained that he could do a better job at the helm than I could.

Bryan spoke up next. "We're asking that John retire immediately and that Verne be named CEO," he said.

So there it was, twenty-three pairs of heels were dug in on both sides. Nothing short of capitulation or all-out war was going to change things. We were at an impasse.

The directors met for several hours, without Verne or myself being present. After all that time, the meeting adjourned without the board taking any action. A total stalemate. The First Chicago faction wanted me out, that was clear, but as time would tell they were reluctant to throw their full support behind Verne.

So the board recommended that Verne and I get together and come up with a solution. That would be like asking oil and water to mix. In my heart I knew that was never going to happen, so of course I was greatly discouraged. More like despondent, really. I was convinced that the company was on the verge of falling apart.

Afterwards I told Bob that the outcome was a bunch of baloney (or words to that effect) and that a reconciliation was not in the cards. There was only one way forward.

"Bob, I've decided to quit tomorrow morning," I said.

"Whoa!" he replied. "You can't quit. If you quit, we're not going to have any leverage. Don't do anything. And besides, how are you going to tell your father you're quitting!"

That last comment stopped me cold. Bob knew me, and he knew father, and one thing that father would not turn his back on was a good fight—especially if he thought he occupied the high ground. "McCoys aren't quitters!" I could imagine him saying, springing from his lounge chair and looking for a First Chicago board member to throttle.

Bob was absolutely right. He was the level-headed strategic thinker I needed at this moment. If I had resigned abruptly, the board would have had no recourse but to make Verne CEO and the whole company might have failed in six months. I needed to hang on for the right outcome.

I flew to Columbus for a change of scenery and to formulate my plans. Over the next few days, Bob and I worked out the broad strokes of what would eventually transpire. I would step down, Verne would be named interim CEO, and the board would agree to conduct an outside search for a permanent CEO. John R. Hall, a Bank One director and retired chairman and CEO of Ashland Inc., a specialty chemical company and maker of Valvoline products, would become nonexecutive chairman of Bank One until a new and permanent CEO was in place. A twelve-year veteran of the Bank One board (mostly predating the First Chicago acquisition), Hall would also lead the CEO search committee.

Bill Boardman, whose title was senior EVP and who had been running First USA for nearly three months, would become a corporate director (taking my vacated seat on the board) and be promoted to vice chairman.

I was falling on my sword, which is never easy for a CEO, but what satisfied me about the arrangement was that people I trusted and respected—Bob Walter, John Hall and Bill Boardman—would be running the company (with

Verne, of course) and leading the search for a permanent CEO. That was something I could feel good about at a time when good feelings were hard to come by.

So who exactly was this John Hall? A native of West Virginia, John spoke r-e-a-l s-l-o-w, occasionally stuttered and was also hard of hearing. Based on appearances alone, I'm certain the First Chicago folks dismissed him completely as just another Banc One rube.

What they didn't know, and even I didn't fully appreciate at the time, was that this former Vanderbilt lineman (a second-team football All-American) was as tough and gritty as they came. Until you go into war, you don't really know how your bunk mates are going to perform in battle. John Hall was a warrior.

He threw himself into the chairman's role, even finding an apartment and moving to Chicago for the duration of the mission, which included providing oversight to Verne, running board meetings and leading the search for a new CEO. John was in the office every day. I think John's zeal for the role surprised a lot of the First Chicago people, who fully expected this retired oilman to be a distant caretaker at best. Despite their best efforts to ignore him, John placed himself squarely in the center of their universe and wouldn't budge.

Years later, Bob Walter commented: "It's interesting that your grandfather John Hall McCoy started this banking dynasty and it took a John Hall to preserve the Bank One legacy."

CHAPTER TWENTY-TWO

End Game

$f$or me, the hardest part was yet to come: telling Father what I had decided. Still feisty at 87, it was not in that man's DNA to back down. He would have thrown a punch at Rocky Marciano if he thought he could land it. Even though Bank One had been a public company for decades, owned by shareholders worldwide, it still bore the stamp of three generations of Mc-Coys. His father had guided City National through the Great Depression and ultimately died at his desk, while my father had transformed a banking runt into the pick of the litter through innovation and execution. No, this news was not going to sit well, and I knew it.

I went to Father's house and we sat down to talk, like we had so many times before. Throughout my career, there was nothing I wouldn't tell Father. I could always confide in him. Fifteen years before he would have been part of the discussion. He would have been my Bob Walter. However, on this day I was not there for counsel; I was there to deliver news. Father never wasted words when he spoke to me, and neither did I in this case.

"Dad, I want you to know that I've decided to step down. I think it's the best thing for the bank."

We looked at each other for what seemed like a long time, and each of us nodded ever so slowly. His disappointment was palpable. Yet because he was so far removed from the day-to-day operation of the company at this point, there was no effort on his part to convince me otherwise. Even if he had, it would not have made a difference. My mind was certainly made up, and by the time I told him, Bob Walter was making the deal with First Chicago. There was no turning back.

"I hoped it wasn't true," he later told a journalist. As for our First Chicago partners, "They didn't treat him right, any way around," he concluded, something I couldn't argue with. Thanks, Pops.

To my great relief, our proposal satisfied the First Chicago faction. They had my head, which was their primary goal, and they probably felt that they could disregard Hall. But he was clever as a whip. He was not taking a backseat to anyone, and that came as a surprise to some of the First Chicago people.

Two days before I left the company, I called Jamie Dimon to let him know what was about to transpire, and what it meant for him. He was surprised that things had unraveled so fast.

"I'm still convinced you're the best person to take this job," I said. "There's going to be a search for a permanent replacement, and I'd like for you to get the job, but for your own sake, don't tell anyone that we've been in contact. That would be the kiss of death for you." I sincerely believed that if word got out that Jamie was seen as "my guy" or that we had even spoken, that he

◄ *Previous page:* Walking away from Bank One was not easy for me personally but ultimately in the best interests of the bank, which was left in very capable hands.

could potentially be disqualified by those on the search committee who were not fond of me. And that would be a shame. There was no second choice as far as I was concerned.

The following day was a Monday, so I used much of the day to meet individually with all my direct reports and some other key people to let them know what was about to transpire, swearing everyone to secrecy. When that was finished the pieces were all in place. Tomorrow couldn't come fast enough, I remember feeling.

On Tuesday, December 21, 1999, I tendered my formal resignation to the Bank One board. The whole thing took maybe five minutes. I walked in and said, "This is a great company and it has a great future. I'm not pleased that I'm leaving but I'm satisfied with the plan. As long as you live up to the plan I'm prepared to resign, and will do so. "

No one said a word. It was done.

I got up, left the room and headed straight to my office. Within a half hour I was headed to my apartment, and later that day on my way to Columbus. Jane and I flew there on the company plane, my last trip on that thing. We had conducted a lot of business in the air for Bank One, but this felt very different.

Jane and I didn't say much, and it was obvious that she was concerned about the toll all this was taking on me. And I felt awful about all that she had been through as well. I didn't want her worrying about me. "I'm the CEO," I remember saying, trying to explain what had just transpired. "When things are going well, I look good. When they go badly, I'm out. That's how it works." I don't know if that helped, but it was true.

My overwhelming feeling was one of relief. I was satisfied that we had come to the best conclusion that we could come to, that Verne was not going to get to run the bank and that we would have the CEO search. My hope was that Jamie was going to be the guy.

We still owned a house in the German Village section of Columbus, a wonderful neighborhood of old homes with courtyards and gardens tightly spaced on brick streets. We had arranged for some of our closest friends to stop by that evening for dinner and some drinks. It was a nice place to be.

Under the headline, "McCoy Quits Bank One; Leadership Issue Simmers," the *American Banker* reported the events this way the next morning:

> Bank One Corp. chairman and chief executive officer John B. McCoy, under fire for several months amid a series of earnings disappointments, announced his resignation Tuesday.
>
> The move, including Mr. McCoy's departure from the banking company's board, took effect immediately and left President Verne G. Istock as acting CEO, pending a search for a permanent replacement.
>
> The installation of an interim CEO is certain to raise further questions about Chicago-based Bank One's leadership, strategic direction, and future as an independent company. In a prepared statement, the company said it would give itself a few months to find a successor to Mr. McCoy.

Then the writer digressed from the financial implications to acknowledge the human element of the story:

> The departure of Mr. McCoy ends a banking dynasty that began in 1935 when his grandfather, John Hall McCoy, joined the Bank One predecessor City National Bank and Trust Co. John B. McCoy's father, John G., took over management of the bank in 1958 and reigned for almost 30 years, retiring as chairman in 1987.
>
> The just-departed CEO helped build the bank from an Ohio-centered regional bank to a company with operations stretching across the United States. Mr. McCoy was not available for comment Tuesday, but market watchers said it was a sad ending to a promising, at times stellar, career.

I don't disagree with any of it, but would add this thought: Sad for me, yes, but plenty of blue sky ahead for Bank One, its employees and shareholders, of which I remained a significant one. With my departure, the healing process could begin.

The CEO search committee was headed by Hall, who partnered with Jim Crown, a legacy director from First Chicago, and four other outside directors. The committee hired the executive search firm Russell Reynolds to help compile a list of candidates, which by February 2000 was pared to a handful.

In addition to Verne, who wanted the job on a permanent basis and had support among some former First Chicago board members, the serious contenders were David Coulter, former CEO of BankAmerica; Lewis Coleman, former chief financial officer at BankAmerica; Texas Commerce Bank CEO Marc Shapiro; and Jamie Dimon. They all were experienced bankers with something to offer and each could make a strong case that they were the right person for the job.

But by the beginning of March, Dimon was emerging as the committee's leading candidate. First and foremost, he had impressed the search group with his record of achievement under Weill at both Travelers and Citigroup. At forty-four, he was recognized as a rising star in the industry with relevant experience in turning around ailing financial services companies. And finally, he was out of a job, available and ready to go.

The committee's selection of Jamie required ratification by the board. As a courtesy, Hall called me the day before the meeting to fill me in on particulars. I told him it was a great outcome. "Jamie is the right guy," I assured Hall.

While some former First Chicago board members wanted to hold out for Verne and argued his case, the end result was never in doubt. Jamie would get the job, and Verne would retain the title of president. On March 27, 2000, Bank One introduced James "Jamie" Dimon as the company's new chairman and CEO.

We had our man.

I called to offer congratulations and my full support. "Whatever I can do to help, just call me any time," I insisted. He said he was humbled by the opportunity to run the nation's fourth-largest bank with more than 80,000 employees, and excited about the future. "I'd like to sit down and get your thoughts on the bank," he replied, so we arranged for him to come to my apartment in Chicago for breakfast a few weeks into his tenure as CEO.

We spoke candidly between bites of English muffins, covering a number of issues ranging from regulators and competitors to Bank One lines of business and personnel. To me his two biggest challenges would be cleaning up the remaining issues at First USA and closing the rift between the First Chicago and Bank One factions. The repair work at First USA was well underway, so I offered my assessment of who he could count on and who might be an obstacle going forward. What he did with the information would be up to him. (About a year later we met for a similar breakfast. "John," Jamie confided, "I have to tell you that you were 95 percent right in your assessments. But I had to prove to myself what you were telling me was correct." Of course he did; there is no other way.)

With Jamie's hiring, the end was near for Verne. Four months into Jamie's tenure, it was announced that Verne, 59, who had retained the title of president and served on the board, would be retiring at the end of September after 37 years with the bank and its predecessors. CFO Rosholt also was shown the door, followed by the departure of three commercial banking executives. Like any good CEO, Jamie had a right to put the people he was comfortable with in places of authority.

Verne was not alone in exiting the board. Bank One announced that five other directors would be leaving "voluntarily" with him, as Jamie reconfigured the unwieldy and divided group of nineteen to a more manageable thirteen. As terms expired, Jamie would also be able to nominate new directors of his choosing, eliminating what remained of the "us vs. them" mentality of former First Chicago and Banc One factions.

Finally, Jamie wisely spent significant time traveling the country to introduce himself to Bank One employees and customers. There really is no substitute for a face-to-face introduction. That personal touch was so important for me whenever Bank One entered a new market, be it in small-town Ohio or Phoenix, Arizona. I'll never forget my first visit to our new Texas headquarters in Dallas after we acquired MCorp. All those demoralized but dedicated employees, peering into the open atrium of their gleaming downtown headquarters, waiting to hear something hopeful from their new leader.

Jamie held employee events at Bank One Ballpark in Phoenix and other cities in that first month. In Chicago he hosted a very large employee gathering at the historic Chicago Theater. His theme throughout: This is still a great franchise and together we can fix it.

The new CEO visited Columbus at the end of his first week on the job, telling about 2,000 employees that all of them, regardless of their rank, were equal in his eyes, if they had good ideas. He also placed a courtesy call to Father, which I know was appreciated. "I wanted him to know I was thrilled to be here," Jamie told *The Columbus Dispatch*. "I said, 'Your son has built a fabulous institution, and I hope what I do makes you proud of me.'"

After sixty-five years of McCoys running Bank One, the Dimon era had begun.

Epilogue

A few days after my "early retirement" from Bank One at age fifty-six, Jane and I found ourselves driving to Florida for some decompression. It was the first time in almost a year that I could truly relax. Jane had been stoic and supportive through those toughest times in Chicago, and for that I'll be forever grateful. And she has commented more than once that she "got my boyfriend back" after we stepped away from the limelight. I try to live up to those expectations.

I had always planned on leaving the bank at age sixty, so I wasn't all that far off the mark. But there's no denying that my abrupt exit was not the way an event planner would draw it up. There's something to be said for easing into retirement and methodically passing the torch to your successor. My departure, on the other hand, called to mind a downhill skier clipping the final gate at the end of a very good run. Yes, the bumps and bruises hurt, but nobody died. I walked away under my own power.

I certainly had my opportunities to jump right back in. A number of private equity firms reached out to me about helping them with financial services mergers and acquisitions. I was asked to serve on several boards (I was already on five at the time—AT&T, Battelle Memorial Institute, Cardinal Health, Freddie Mac and the PGA Tour). And a large bank in London contacted me to gauge my interest in serving as CEO. I listened to all the inbound offers, but said no to them all. I didn't have anything to prove, and Jane had specifically forbid me from accepting any job offers for at least six months.

For weeks after my departure, I fielded calls from Bank One colleagues who needed advice on how to navigate their transition to a new CEO. Should they stay or should they go? Careers and livelihoods were on the line and people were nervous. In so many ways it was tougher on them than on me, so I did what I could from the sidelines to help them through it. (A number of my former managers went on to become CEOs of other banks and many others continue to enjoy leading roles at Chase and other financial institutions. Beth Mooney, who ran Bank One Dayton for me, is the current CEO of Cleveland-based KeyCorp, making her the highest-ranking female bank executive in the country.)

The hardest thing about the way I left was not having the chance to thank the hundreds of people for their years of service and loyalty to the company and to our family. Happily, a few years into my retirement, Jane and I chartered a sailing ship and treated about fifty couples—former Bank One friends and associates ranging from secretaries to board members—to a week-long Caribbean cruise. That was our first real opportunity to reconnect as a group, relive the good times and extend the thank-yous that were in order after all those years.

◄ *Previous page:* I loved my career but there's nothing more important to me than family—wife Jane, daughter Paige Meuse, sister Jinny, son John T. and daughter Tracy Gillette—pictured here on the sidelines of an Ohio State football game in Ohio Stadium. Go Bucks!

Many people have asked why I chose to step aside rather than fight the First Chicago faction of the board, considering that our side had the votes to prevail. My own father even expressed that sentiment in private and in public. It's a fair question and my answer is simple: The company was more important than any individual, including me. History has borne that out.

In 2004, Jamie Dimon negotiated the sale of Bank One to J.P. Morgan Chase, creating the nation's second-largest bank with $1.1 trillion in assets, just a hair smaller than Citicorp at that time. The $58 billion deal combined Bank One's 1,800 branches mainly in the nation's midsection with Chase's 530 in the New York area and Texas, and Chase's relatively small credit card business with First USA, still a market leader despite its previous stumbles.

So why did Jamie and the Bank One board agree to sell? For the same reason that more than 100 banks agreed to sell to me: those two companies would be stronger together than apart. From a leadership perspective, Chase had no clear succession plan for replacing CEO William B. Harrison Jr., who was 60 at the time of the merger. The deal called for Harrison to run the combined companies but cede the CEO role to Jamie (age 47) after two years, with Harrison remaining as chairman. Until then Jamie would be president and chief operating officer of the much larger company.

Though the merger made total sense for Bank One from a competitive standpoint, there was widespread concern in Columbus that the merger and resulting move of the corporate headquarters from Chicago to New York City would relegate the city to second- or third-tier status, vulnerable to layoffs as important work was shifted to other regions. In fact, just the opposite happened. When I left the bank in 1999 there were about 8,000 Bank One employees in Columbus, and I'm pleased to say that the number has grown to nearly three times that level.

These are not just clerical or call-center positions, though there is some of that to be sure. The Columbus area is home to employees who support all of Chase's lines of business and corporate groups. The largest segment in Columbus is Consumer and Community Banking, which includes the

Chase branch and ATM network, small-business banking and the mortgage business, which together represent the core of Bank One's former retail banking business.

In 2011, in part to underscore his commitment to the region, Jamie held Chase's annual shareholders meeting in Columbus rather than New York. The chosen venue was the McCoy Center, the 2-million-square-foot complex with more than 10,000 workers, the largest Chase office building in the world. (Allow me to beam a little here—it was my decision in the mid-1990s to build the McCoy Center, which we originally called the Polaris Centers of Commerce in the city's northern suburbs as a way to supplement our downtown workforce and allow for future growth. And there's more room still.)

Looking beyond Columbus, J.P. Morgan Chase, with a market capitalization of $310 billion, assets of $2.4 trillion and more than 235,000 employees in over 100 countries, remains the gold standard among U.S. financial institutions. As a shareholder, I couldn't be happier with that outcome.

So when I think about my career, I judge it less by what has become of John B. McCoy than by what has become of Bank One—rising from a weak number three in Ohio's capital city with Phyllis Diller hawking business, to being an integral part of the nation's largest and most profitable bank. The hard work of three generations of McCoys has not gone unrewarded.

As for me, I'm not one to dwell or second guess. The future has always been my focus. I'm ready for what's next. I loved college, graduate school and my career at Bank One, but I wouldn't want to repeat any of it. Jane and I have been blessed with a wonderful family—three children (Tracy, Paige and John T.) and eight grandchildren at this writing. I've never forgotten that while I was flying around the country buying banks, Janie was running our household and raising our children. Who had the more important job? My opinion on that has changed through the years.

Index

Thomas, Dick, 159, 174, 176
Tolleson, John, 166–171, 189, 200
TransUnion, 73
Travelers Group, 179, 196, 208

U

Uncommon Partnership, 37–38, 40–42, 51,
    141–143, 145
Union 76, 4
Union National Bank, 50
USAA, 124
U.S. Air Force, 60, 62
US Bancorp, 153–155

V

Vague, Dick, 167, 170–172, 183–189, 192–
    193, 197
Valley National Bank, *134*, 135–136, 172, 185
Valley National Corp., 136
Valvoline, 202
Visa, 30, 34–35
Vitale, David, 179–180, 193
Volcker, Paul, 90

W

Wachovia, 153
Wachtell, Lipton, Rosen & Katz, 198
Wall Street, 92, 99, 111, 113, 128, 131, 137,
    139, 143, 170, 186, 189, 191
Wall Street Journal, 114, 131, 190
Walter, Bob, 192–193, 200–203, 205
Walton, Sam, 86, 88
Warren, Ellen, 182
WCLT-AM, 26
Weill, Sandy, 195–197
Wells Fargo, 120, 123, 136, *150*, 151, 153–155
Wexner, Leslie, 35
White, George, 5, 8, 10
Williams College, 57–58
Winters Bank, 51
Winters, Jonathan, 51
Winters National Bank & Trust, 51
Wolfe, John F., 177
World War II, 15–16, 18
Wright, Orville, 51
Wright, Wilbur, 51